The Incredibles Drawing Book Step-by-Step

Learn How to Draw Popular Characters from the Incredibles with the Easy and Fun Guide

Table of Contents

Learn How to Draw Popular Characters from the Incredibles with the Easy and Fun Guide 1

Introduction 10

How to draw Mr. Incredible 11

.... 12

1. Draw one horizontal curved oval shape and three vertical ones. 12
It will be the hair. 12

.... 13

2. Draw already. To do this, draw an oval shape inside 13
which we draw an arc. 13

.... 14

3. We connect the ears with a rectangular arc. 14

.... 15

4. Draw a rectangular shape below. This will be the neck. 15

.... 16

5. On the right and left of the neck we draw an arc. 16
It will be the shoulders. 16

.... 17

6. Draw a horizontal oval shape. It will be an emblem. 17

.... 18

7. Draw two parallel curved arcs to the right and to the left. 18
It will be hands. 18

.... 19

8. Draw two parallel lines that end in a rectangular shape. 19
Inside this form, draw four short lines. Repeat the same 19
for the second hand. 19

.... 20

9. Inside each hand we draw a horizontal arc. We add two vertical 20
lines of the trunk. 20

.... 21

10. Draw a horizontal arc. Below this arc, draw two more arcs connected together. They will be cowards. .. 21

.... 22

11. Below we draw two connected Oval forms. The same shape is drawn on the other side. It will be legs... 22

.... 23

12. At the bottom we add rectangular forms of feet. Above draw 23
the horizontal arcs of shoes. 23

.... 24

13. Inside the head, draw two parallel curved lines. In the center at the top, add two short lines. It will be a mask. 24

14. For the mouth, draw a horizontal arc. To the right and left of this arc draw a line. For the nose, draw a rectangular shape. 25
.... 26
15. For the eyes inside the horizontal oval shape, we draw an oval shape of smaller size. Same for the second eye. 26
.... 27
16. Done! Great job. Now go to the color. 27
.... 28
17. The body of Mr. Incredible is ocher, red-black clothes. 28
.... 29
18. Next we add shadows and light to make 29
Mr. Incredible volumetric. 29
.... 30
19. Colored version 30

How to draw Elastigirl 31
.... 32
1. Draw two arcs connected together. It will be the hair. 32
.... 33
2. Inside the formed form, we draw two connected arcs. 33
Add curved lines to the left. This will be the face lines. 33
.... 34
3. Draw a rectangular shape. This will be the neck. 34
.... 35
4. Right and left of the neck draw lines. This is the line of hands. 35
.... 36
5. On the left we draw three connected arcs. There are two on the right. 36
We add two arcs of the body. 36
.... 37
6. Left and right draw a rectangular shape of the hands. 37
The left form ends with five oval forms connected together. 37
On the right is four. 37
.... 38
7. In the center we draw a rectangular shape. It will be a belt. 38
.... 39
8. Draw two arcs connected at the end. 39
.... 40
9. Add two rectangular shapes. It will be legs. 40
.... 41
10. Draw on the left two curved parallel lines that are connected at the end to each other. On the right we draw similar lines which are connected by means of two connected rectangular forms. 41
.... 42
11. Drawing the logo. To do this, draw a horizontal oval shape. 42
.... 43
12. Draw two curved lines on the face. It will be a mask. 43

.... 44
13. Below the mask, draw a curved line of the nose. Below the nose draw three connected at the ends of the arc of the mouth. 44
.... 45
14. For the eyes, draw an oval shape inside which 45
we draw an oval shape smaller than the size. We draw the same for the second eye. 45
.... 46
15. Done! Great job. Now go to the color. 46
.... 47
16. Body of Elastigirl is ocher, clothing is red-black, hair is brown. 47
.... 48
17. Next, we add shadows and light to make 48
the Elastigirl volumetric. 48
.... 49
18. Colored version 49

How to draw Violet Parr *50*

.... 51
1. Draw two connected triangular shapes. It will be the hair. 51
.... 52
2. I draw ears. To do this, draw rectangular shapes inside 52
which draw arcs. 52
.... 53
3. We connect the ears with the help of an arc. From each 53
ear we draw a vertical line. 53
.... 54
4. Below our heads, we draw a rectangular shape 54
of the neck. From the neck to the right and left, draw an arc 54
that is rounded at the end. 54
.... 55
5. Drawing the inner surface of the hands. To do this, ... 55
draw the arc to the right and to the left. 55
.... 56
6. Draw two arcs in the center which are connected by parallel lines. This will be the body and belt lines. ... 56
.... 57
7. Add curved rectangular shapes to the right and left. 57
.... 58
8. Draw three connected arcs. 58
.... 59
9. For the legs we draw curved long oval forms connected at the end. 59
At the bottom of the left foot, add a rectangular shape of the heel. 59
.... 60
10. In the upper part of the legs we draw lines. 60
.... 61
11. For the emblem, draw a horizontal oval shape 61
.... 62

12. Inside the head, draw a rectangular shape. It will be a mask. 62

13. Below the mask, draw a curved line of the nose. Below the nose draw a horizontal line of the mouth. ... 63

14. For the eyes, draw a horizontal oval shape inside 64
which we draw a circular shape of the pupil. Repeat the same 64
for the second eye. 64

15. Done! Great job. Now go to the color. 65

16. Body of Violet is light pink, clothes are red-black, hair is black. 66

17. Next we add shadows and light to make Violet volumetric. 67

18. Colored version 68

How to draw Dash 69

1. Draw three connected oval forms. It will be the hair. 70

2. Inside we draw two connected arcs. 71

3. Drawing the ear. To do this, we draw an arc from the left, drawing an arc of a smaller size. 72

4. We connect the ear with the hair line. To do this, draw 73
an oval face line. 73

5. Below our heads draw a short vertical line and a horizontal line of shoulders. 74

6. On the right, we draw two connected rectangular forms. 75
Inside less form draw four arcs. It will be a hand. 75

7. On the left, we draw a curved rectangular shape 76
of the second hand. 76

8. Draw from the hands of the arc which will be the body. 77

9. We connect the arcs with a horizontal line. From this line down we draw two vertical lines. Below we draw
two connected arcs. 78

10. Draw two rectangular shapes connected at the end. 79
It will be legs. 79

11. In the lower part of the legs we draw horizontal lines. 80
This is the line of shoes. 80

12. For the emblem, draw a horizontal oval shape. 81

.... 82

13. Inside the head, draw a horizontal oval shape. 82

It will be a mask. 82

.... 83

14. Below the mask draw curved lines for the nose. Below the nose, draw the arc ends that point upward. It will be a mouth. 83

.... 84

15. For the eyes, draw a horizontal oval shape inside each shape and 84

draw a vertical arc. 84

.... 85

16. Done! Great job. Now go to the color. 85

.... 86

17. Dash's body is light pink, his clothes are red and black, ... 86

his hair is yellow. 86

.... 87

18. Next, we add shadows and light to make Dash volumetric. 87

.... 88

19. Colored version 88

How to draw Jack-Jack Parr **89**

.... 90

1. Draw a triangular shape. It will be the hair. 90

.... 91

2. Right and left of the hair draw an arc. It will be a head. 91

.... 92

3. Drawing ears. For this, on the right and left, draw a circular shape inside which we draw an arc. 92

.... 93

4. We connect the ears with the help of an arc. 93

.... 94

5. Draw a horizontal line. These will be the lines of hands. 94

.... 95

6. On the right and on the left we draw palms. To do this, draw two connected oval forms. Inside the larger form we hold 4 lines. 95

.... 96

7. Down from the palms we draw a line. Below the palms 96

draw horizontal arcs. 96

.... 97

8. Add two arcs that will be the body. 97

.... 98

9. Draw the circular shape on the left. Up from this form, draw two connected at the beginning of the arc. .. 98

.... 99

10. On the right, we draw a rectangular shape that connects to 99

the body with two parallel lines. This will be the second leg. 99

.... 100

11. Inside the head, draw a horizontal rectangular shape. 100

It will be a mask. 100
.... 101
12. Below the mask draw an arc. It will be a nose. 101
Below the nose draw two arcs connected at the ends. Inside the formed form, draw an arc. It will be a mouth. 101
.... 102
13. To draw an eye inside the oval horizontal shapes draw a round shape. 102
The same way we draw the second eye. 102
.... 103
14. Done! Great job. Now go to the color. 103
.... 104
15. The body of Jack-Jack is light pink, the clothes are red-black, the hair is brown. 104
.... 105
16. Next, we add shadows and light to make Jack-Jack voluminous. 105
.... 106
17. Colored version 106

How to draw Mirage 107
.... 108
1. Draw two connected triangular forms. It will be the hair. 108
.... 109
2. On the left we draw an ear. For this we draw an arc. 109
We connect the hair lines with an oval arc. It will be a head. 109
.... 110
3. Below our heads draw two curved lines. These will be the lines of the neck and shoulders. We connect the lines of shoulders and hair with vertical lines. 110
.... 111
4. We connect the neck lines with two parallel arcs. 111
It will be a decoration. Below we draw two interconnected triangular forms. 111
It will be a dress. 111
.... 112
5. On the right, we draw two parallel straight lines. On the left, draw two curved parallel lines. It will be hands. 112
.... 113
6. Draw two zigzag lines. It will be a dress. 113
.... 114
7. On the right, we draw two rectangular connected forms. 114
This will be the palm of hand. On the left we add a triangular shape of hair. 114
.... 115
8. Draw two straight lines connected together in the beginning. 115
.... 116
9. Draw four curved lines that will be legs. 116
.... 117
10. On the left we draw a rectangular shape. On the right, we draw two connected rectangular forms. It will be shoes. 117
.... 118

11. Add 3 lines of dress. 118

.... 119

12. For the nose, draw a straight rounded end. To draw a mouth draw three connected at each end of the arc. 119

.... 120

13. For the eyes, we draw triangular shapes inside which we draw round shapes. Above the eyes we draw eyebrows. 120

.... 121

14. Done! Great job. Now go to the color. 121

.... 122

15. Body of Mirage is pink, dress violet, hair gray. 122

.... 123

16. Next, we add shadows and light to make 123
the Mirage voluminous. 123

.... 124

17. Colored version 124

How to draw Edna Mode **125**

.... 126

1. Draw the arc ends that are pointing down. It will be the hair. 126

.... 127

2. Draw inside a rectangular shape at the ends of which 127
we draw horizontal lines. 127

.... 128

3. Draw two curved arcs that will be face. To the right and left of the face we hold arches of ears. 128

.... 129

4. Below we draw a rectangular vertical shape. It will be clothes. 129

.... 130

5. Inside we draw two perpendicular lines connected together. 130

.... 131

6. On the right we draw a hand. To do this, we connect two rectangular forms. Below, draw two lines connected to the body. 131

.... 132

7. In the same way, draw the second hand on the left. 132

.... 133

8. Draw four vertical lines that end in rectangular shapes. 133
It will be legs. 133

.... 134

9. Draw two round shapes on the head. It will be glasses. In the center of the glasses draw an arc whose ends are directed down. Inside this arc draw two arcs the size smaller. It will be a nose. 134

.... 135

10. Draw the arc whose ends are directed upwards. 135
It will be a mouth. For the eyes, draw two connected at the ends 135
of the horizontal lines. Inside the formed shapes, draw a short vertical arc. 135

.... 136

11. Done! Great job. Now go to the color. 136

.... 137

12. Edna's body Ocher colors, blue-black clothes, black hair. 137

.... 138

13. Next, we add shadows and light to make Edna voluminous. 138

.... 139

14. Colored version 139

Introduction

Being good at art doesn't happen straight away. In fact, it's likely that you'll make mistakes at first – but that doesn't matter! In fact, it's the best way to learn and improve!

The good news is that this book contains some of the secrets which will help you gain the skills you need. When you learn to draw, it is important to take it one step at a time. That's why the following pages give you step-by-step guidance. This is because when you draw a picture, it isn't perfect immediately – it builds up over time.

This means that not only do you need to draw carefully and bit by bit – you also need to practice a lot. The more times the draw something, the easier it will be to do it again. Eventually you will be able to draw what you like without the instructions!

One tip for learning to draw is that you need to look really carefully at the steps in this book. In fact, some of the best artists spend more time looking at what they are drawing than making marks on the paper! This is called observation. The better you are at observing the instructions, the easier it will be to draw your favorite things. Remember, practice makes perfect – so if you want to create perfect drawings, you'll have to work at it!

How to draw Mr. Incredible

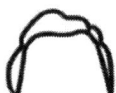

1. Draw one horizontal curved oval shape and three vertical ones. It will be the hair.

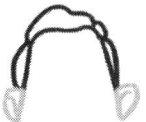

2. Draw already. To do this, draw an oval shape inside which we draw an arc.

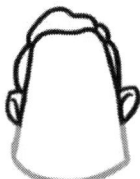

3. We connect the ears with a rectangular arc.

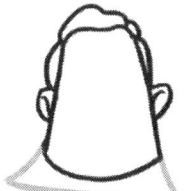

4. Draw a rectangular shape below. This will be the neck.

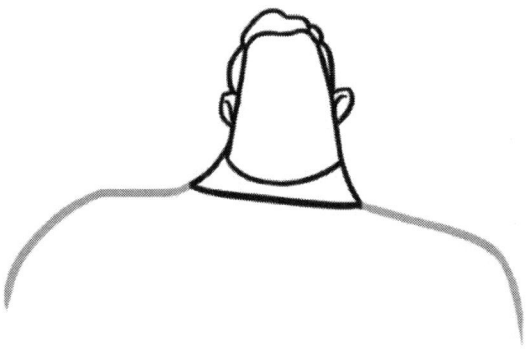

5. On the right and left of the neck we draw an arc.
It will be the shoulders.

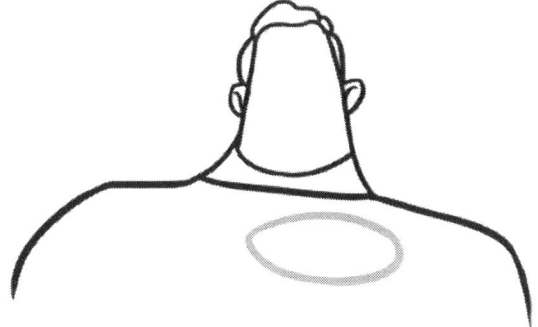

6. Draw a horizontal oval shape. It will be an emblem.

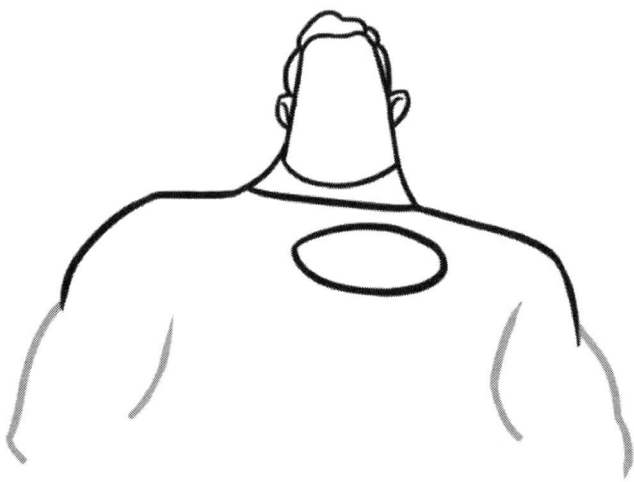

7. Draw two parallel curved arcs to the right and to the left.
It will be hands.

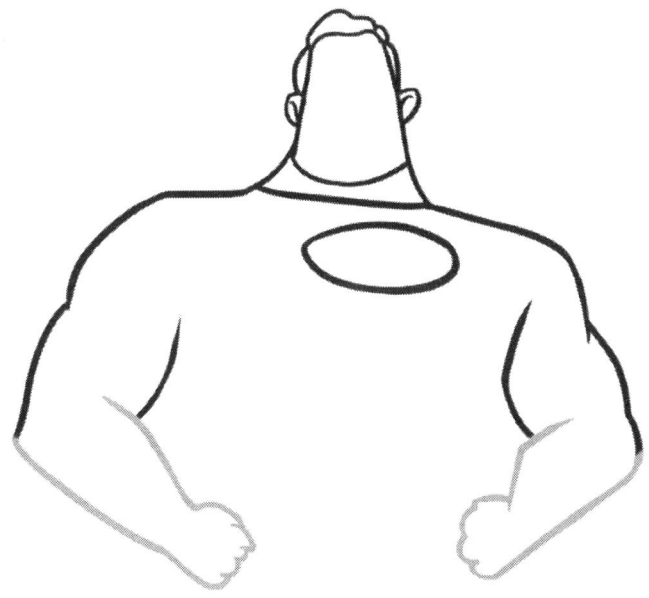

8. Draw two parallel lines that end in a rectangular shape. Inside this form, draw four short lines. Repeat the same for the second hand.

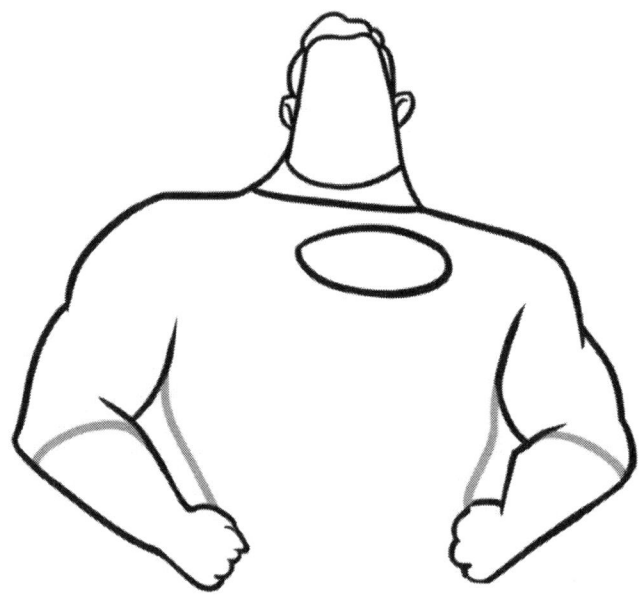

9. Inside each hand we draw a horizontal arc. We add two vertical lines of the trunk.

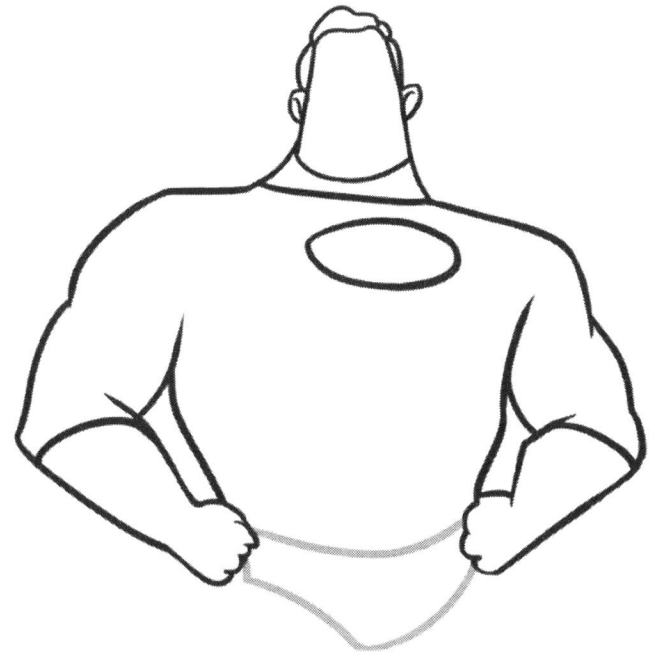

10. Draw a horizontal arc. Below this arc, draw two more arcs connected together. They will be cowards.

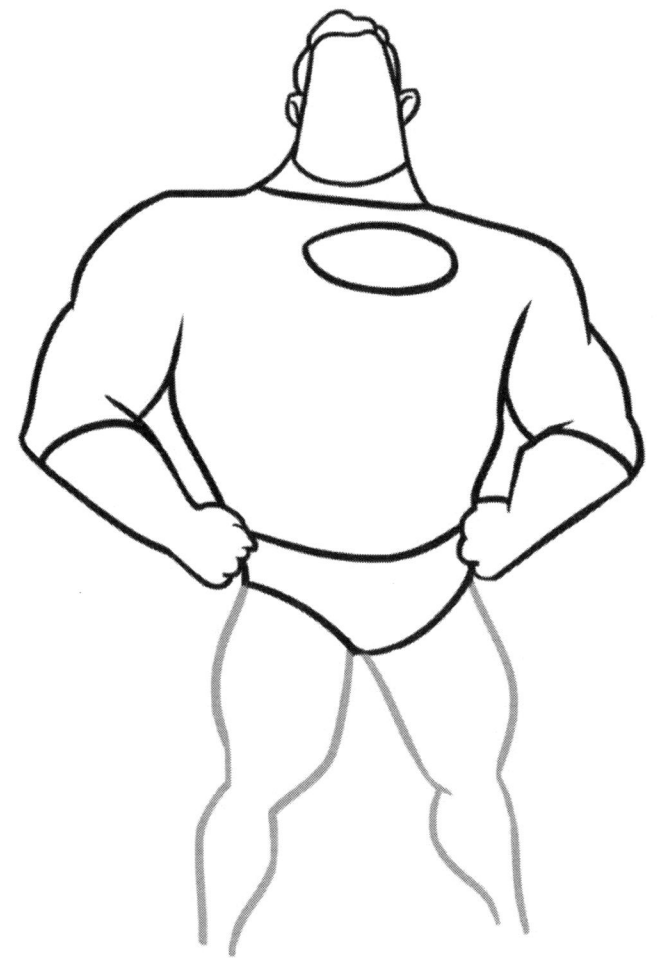

11. Below we draw two connected Oval forms. The same shape is drawn on the other side. It will be legs.

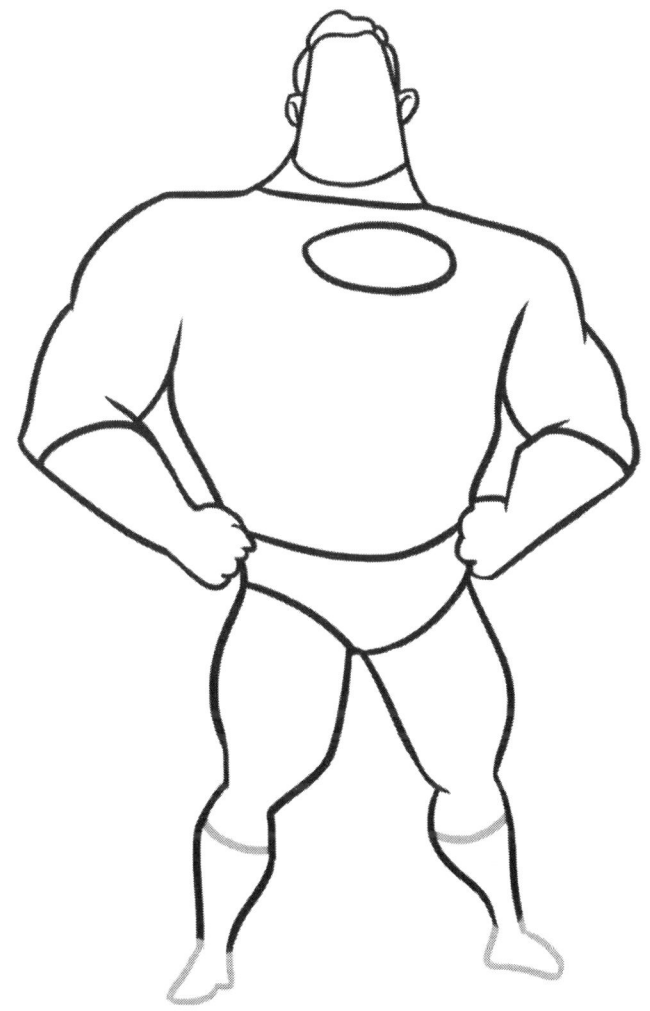

12. At the bottom we add rectangular forms of feet. Above draw the horizontal arcs of shoes.

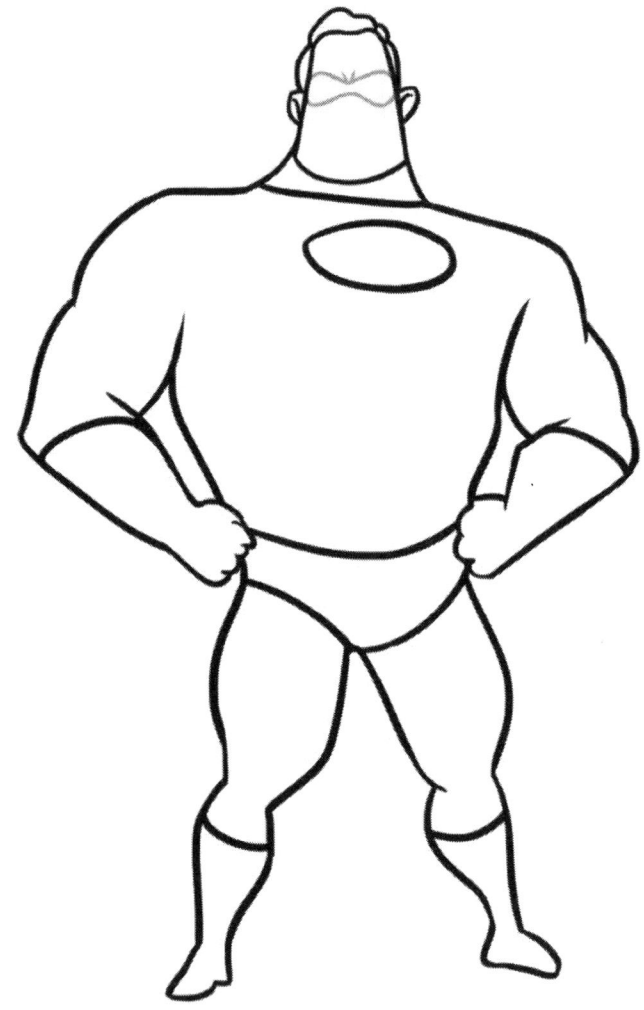

13. Inside the head, draw two parallel curved lines. In the center at the top, add two short lines. It will be a mask.

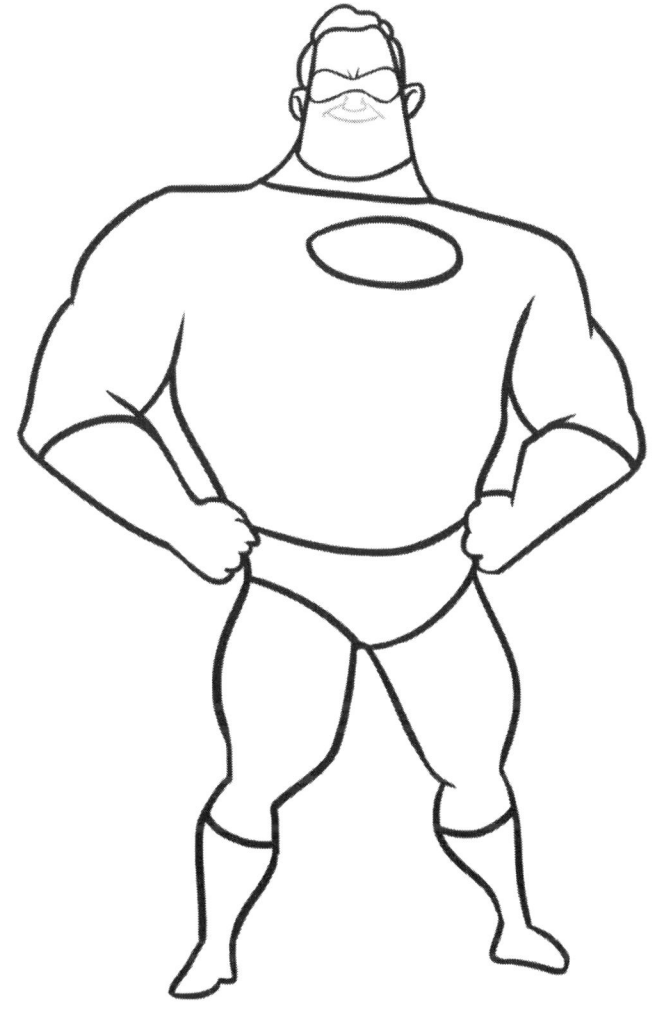

14. For the mouth, draw a horizontal arc. To the right and left of this arc draw a line. For the nose, draw a rectangular shape.

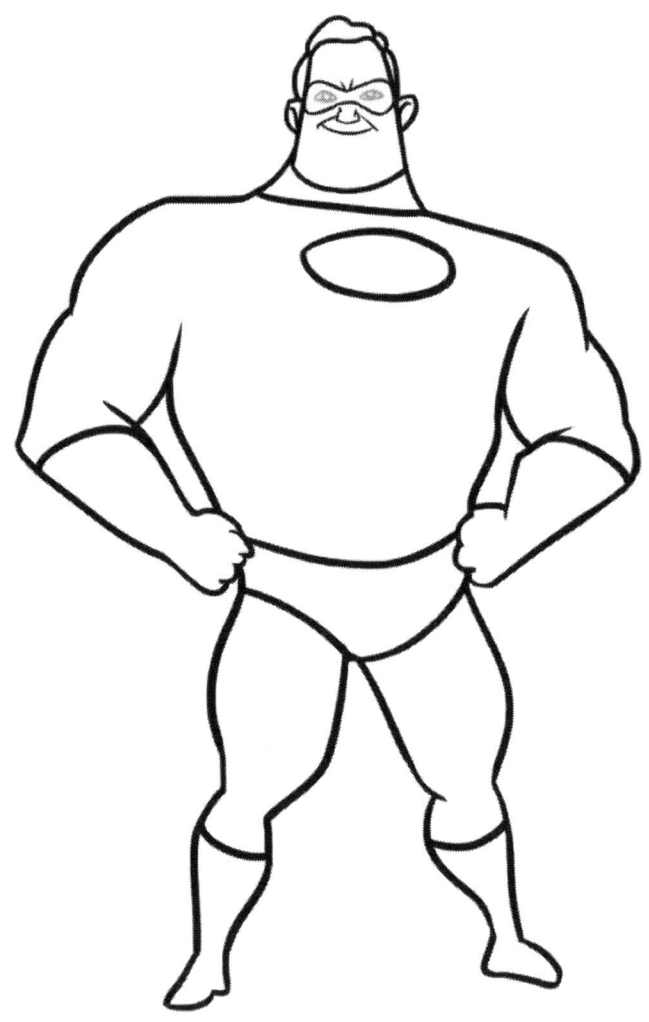

15. For the eyes inside the horizontal oval shape, we draw an oval shape of smaller size. Same for the second eye.

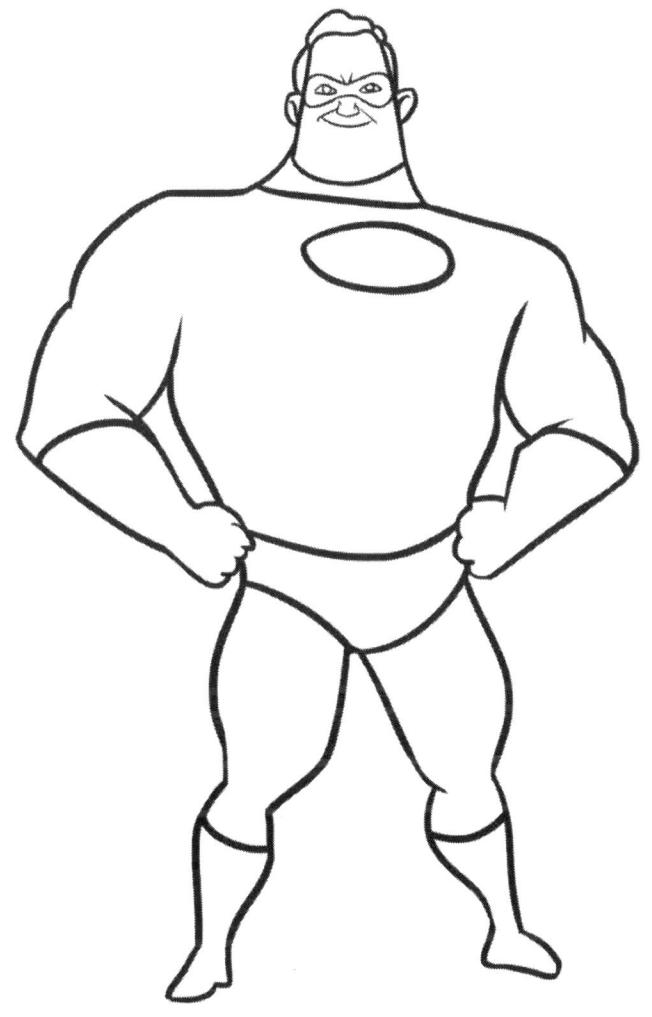

16. Done! Great job. Now go to the color.

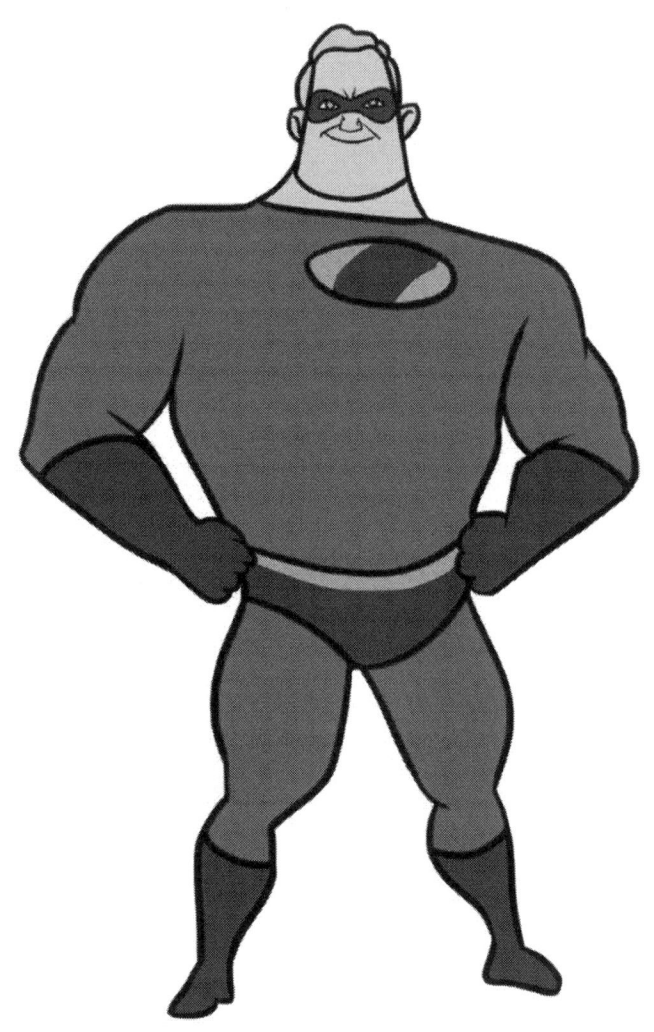

17. The body of Mr. Incredible is ocher, red-black clothes.

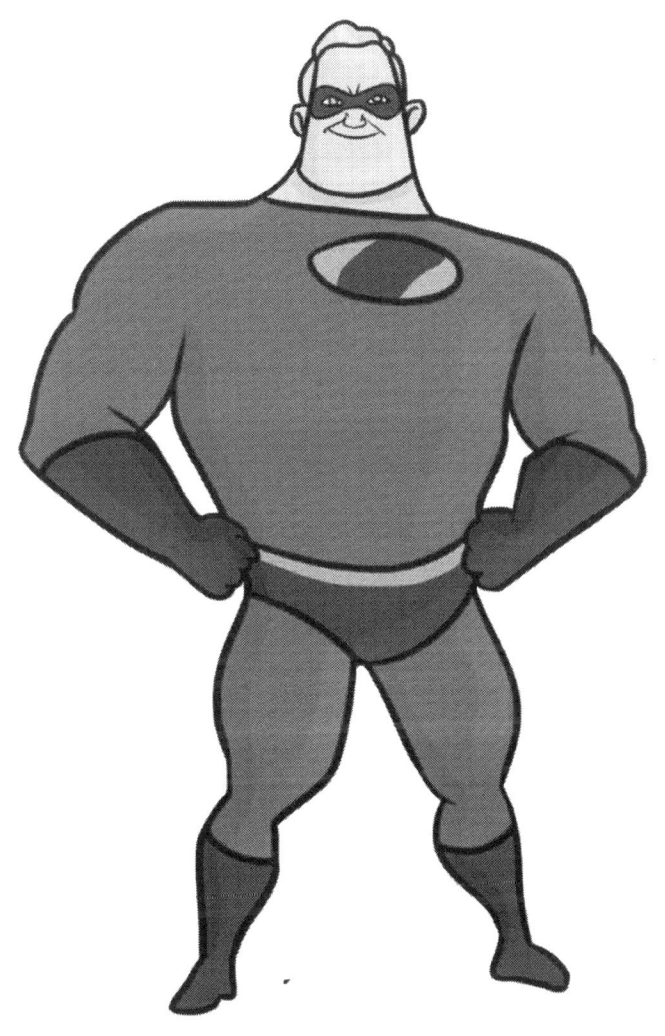

18. Next we add shadows and light to make Mr. Incredible volumetric.

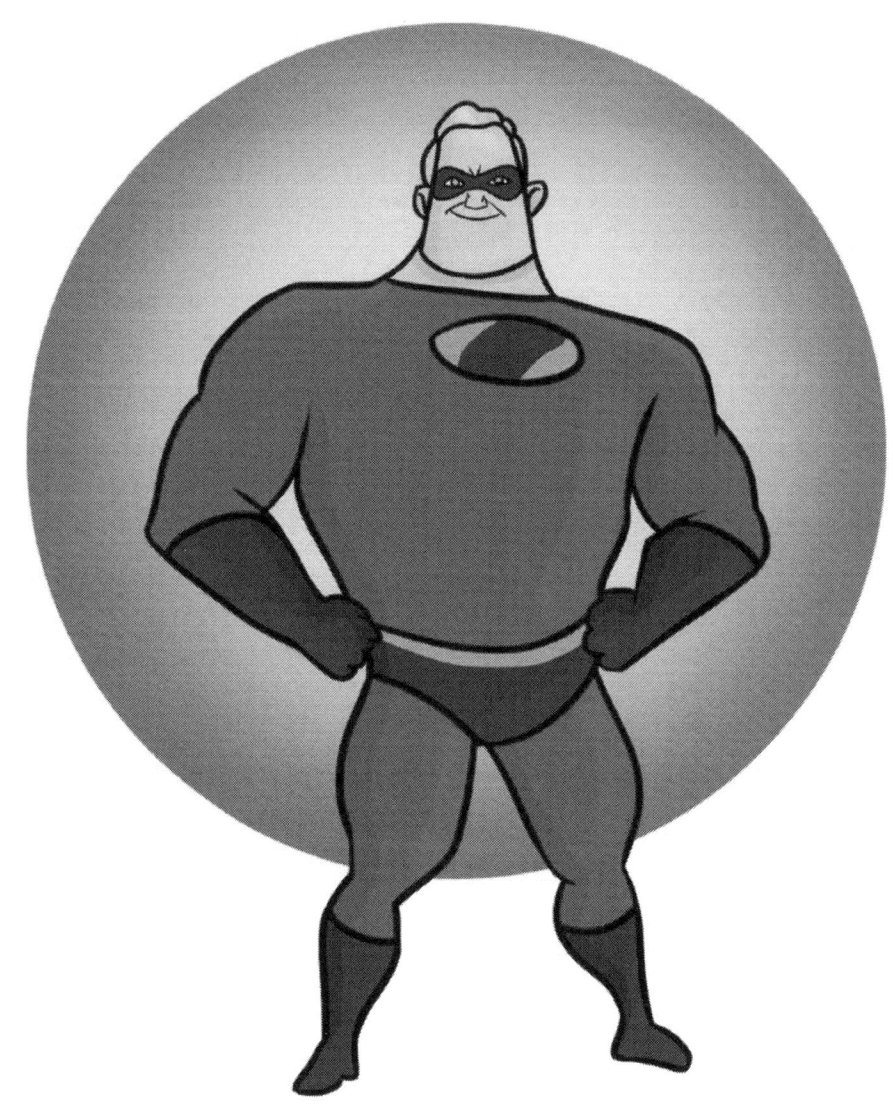

19. Colored version

How to draw Elastigirl

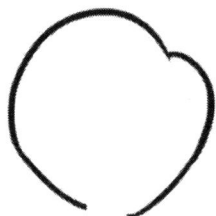

1. Draw two arcs connected together. It will be the hair.

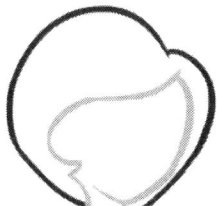

2. Inside the formed form, we draw two connected arcs.
Add curved lines to the left. This will be the face lines.

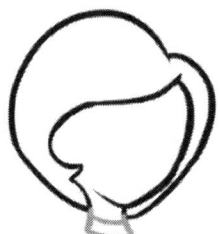

3. Draw a rectangular shape. This will be the neck.

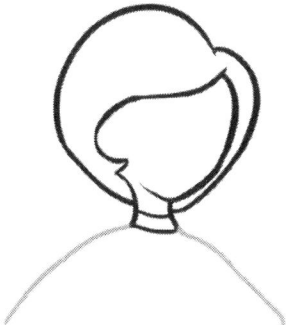

4. Right and left of the neck draw lines. This is the line of hands.

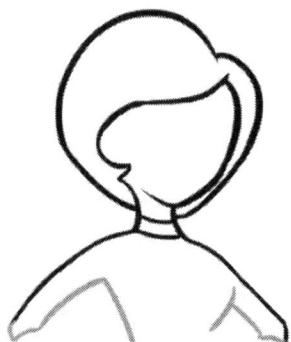

5. On the left we draw three connected arcs. There are two on the right.
We add two arcs of the body.

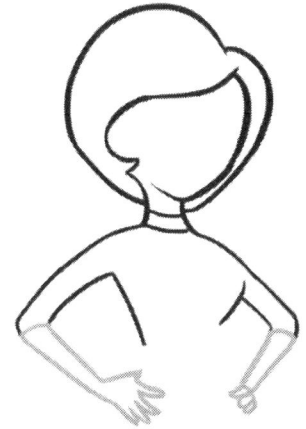

6. Left and right draw a rectangular shape of the hands.
The left form ends with five oval forms connected together.
On the right is four.

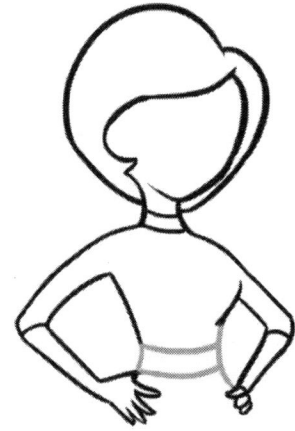

7. In the center we draw a rectangular shape. It will be a belt.

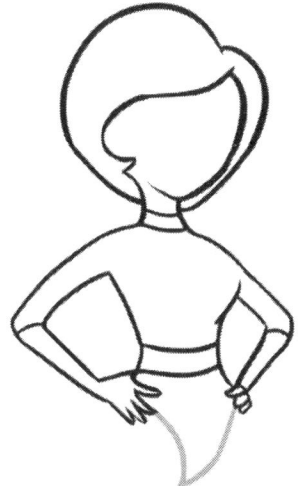

8. Draw two arcs connected at the end.

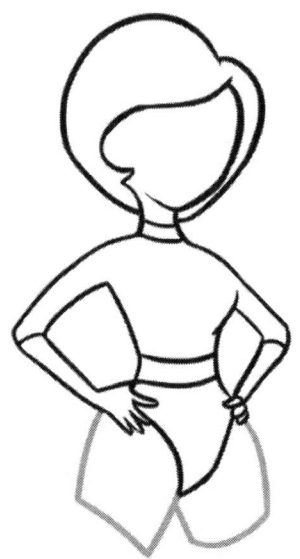

9. Add two rectangular shapes. It will be legs.

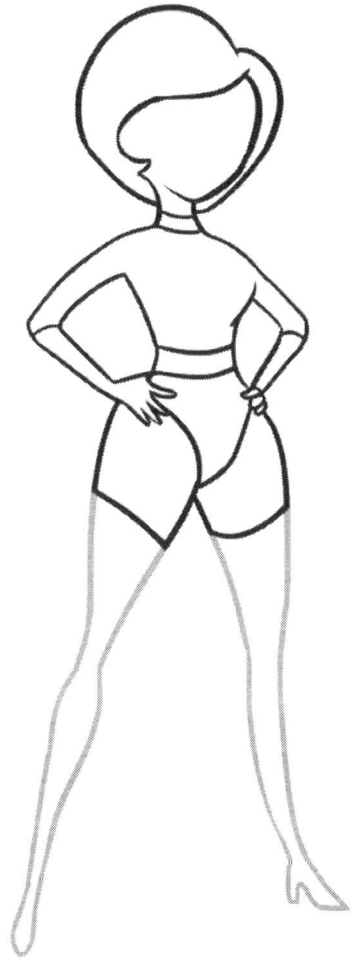

10. Draw on the left two curved parallel lines that are connected at the end to each other. On the right we draw similar lines which are connected by means of two connected rectangular forms.

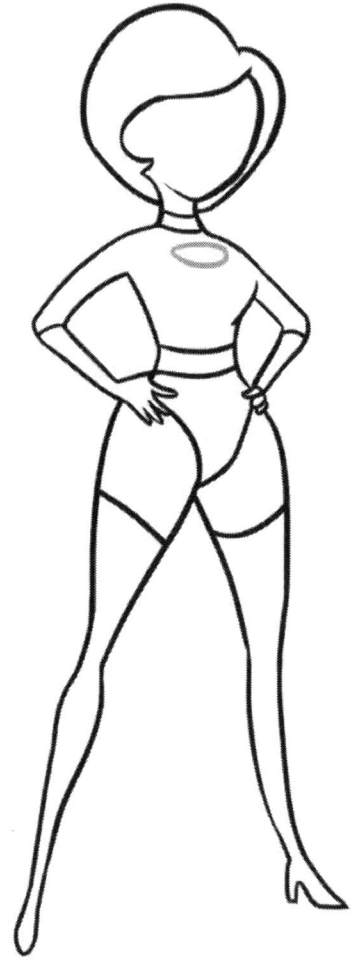

11. Drawing the logo. To do this, draw a horizontal oval shape.

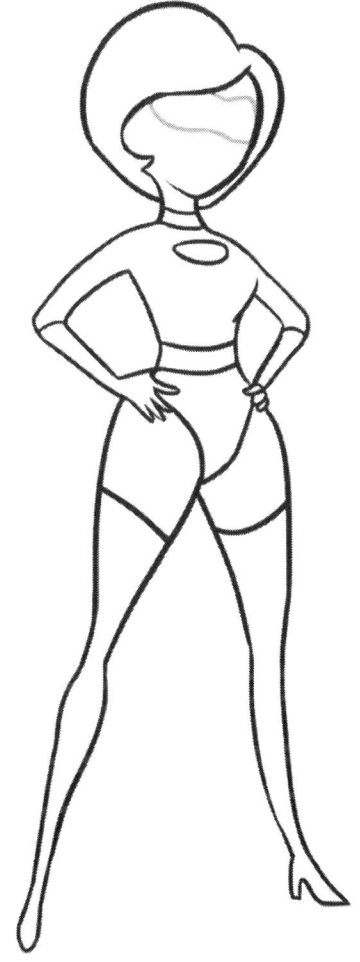

12. Draw two curved lines on the face. It will be a mask.

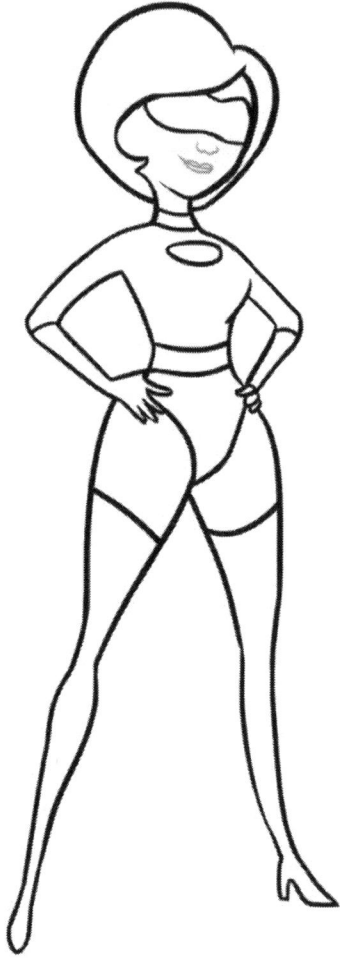

13. Below the mask, draw a curved line of the nose. Below the nose draw three connected at the ends of the arc of the mouth.

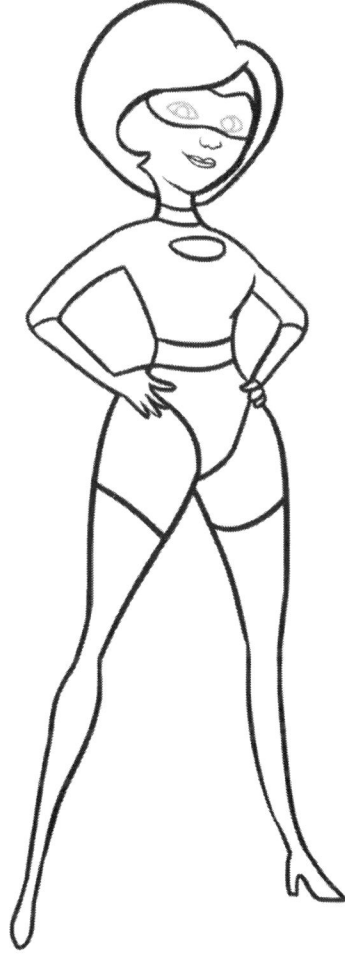

14. For the eyes, draw an oval shape inside which we draw an oval shape smaller than the size. We draw the same for the second eye.

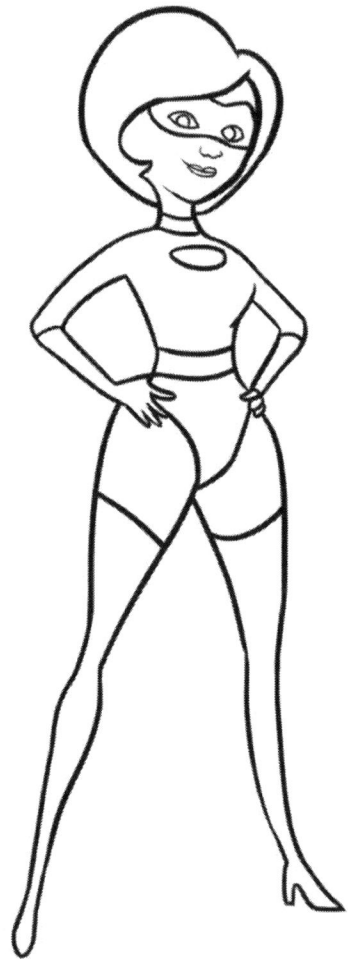

15. Done! Great job. Now go to the color.

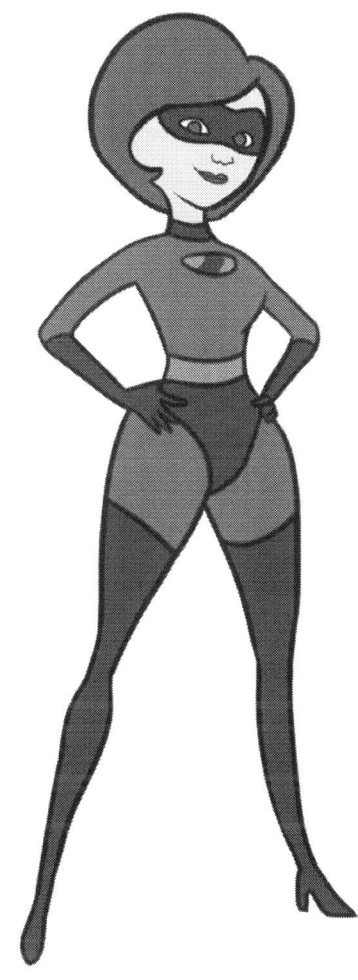

16. Body of Elastigirl is ocher, clothing is red-black, hair is brown.

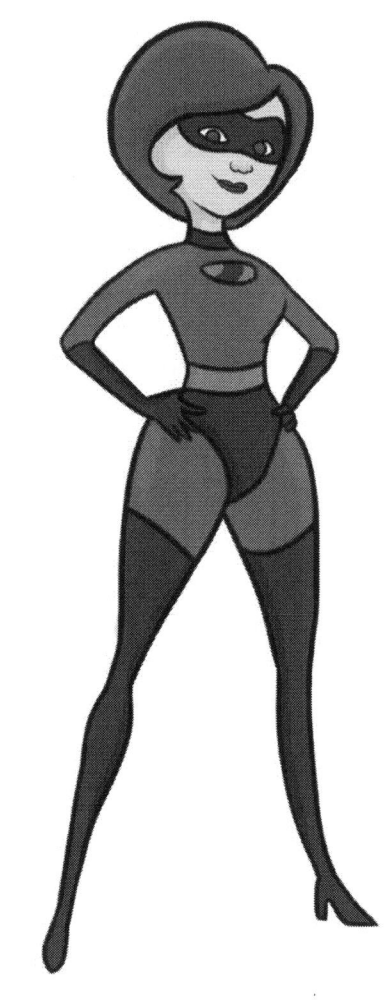

17. Next, we add shadows and light to make the Elastigirl volumetric.

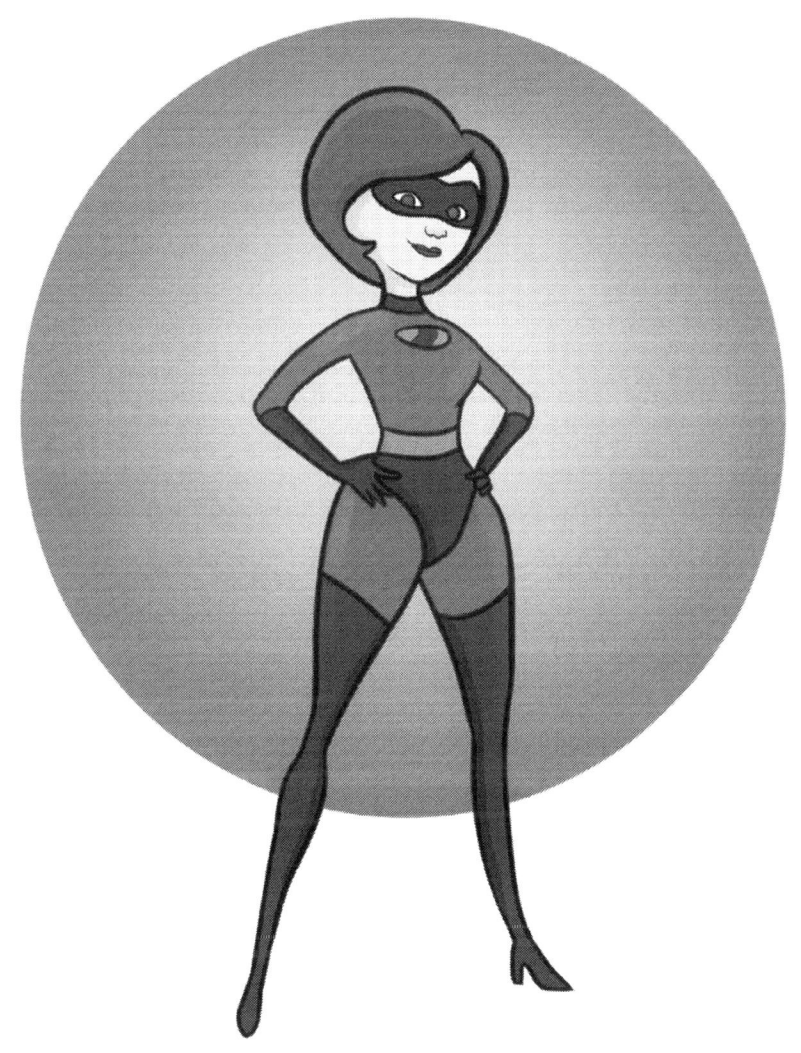

18. Colored version

How to draw Violet Parr

1. Draw two connected triangular shapes. It will be the hair.

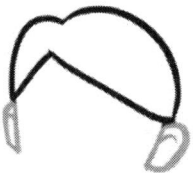

2. I draw ears. To do this, draw rectangular shapes inside which draw arcs.

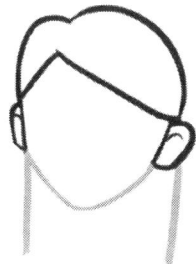

3. We connect the ears with the help of an arc. From each ear we draw a vertical line.

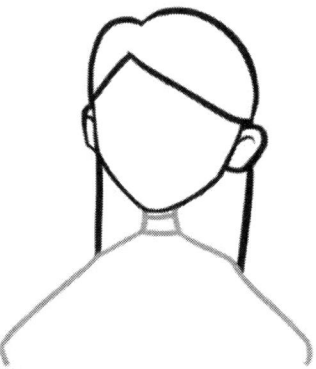

4. Below our heads, we draw a rectangular shape of the neck. From the neck to the right and left, draw an arc that is rounded at the end.

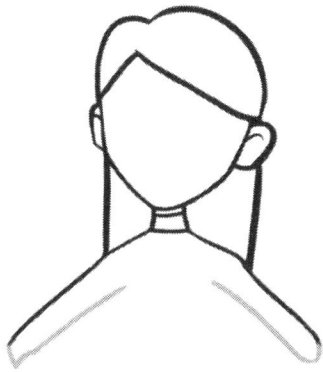

5. Drawing the inner surface of the hands. To do this, draw the arc to the right and to the left.

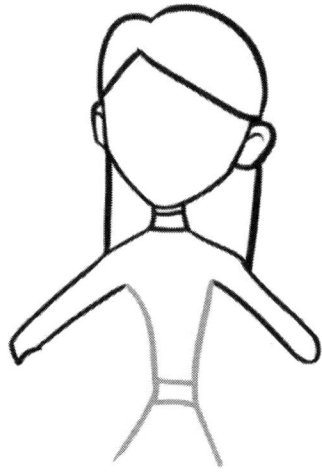

6. Draw two arcs in the center which are connected by parallel lines. This will be the body and belt lines.

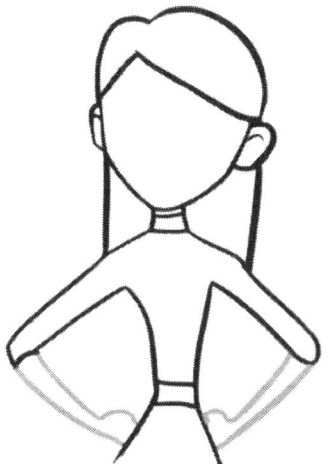

7. Add curved rectangular shapes to the right and left.

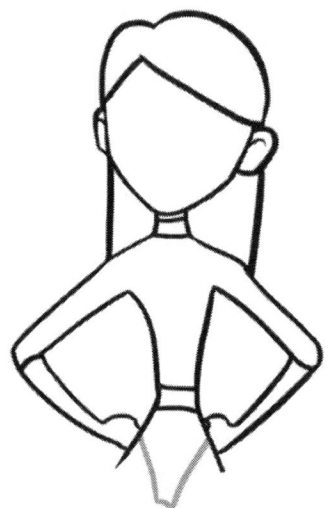

8. Draw three connected arcs.

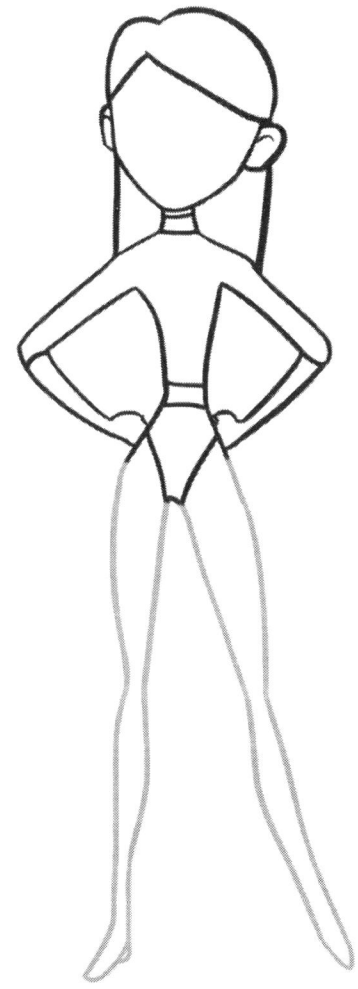

9. For the legs we draw curved long oval forms connected at the end. At the bottom of the left foot, add a rectangular shape of the heel.

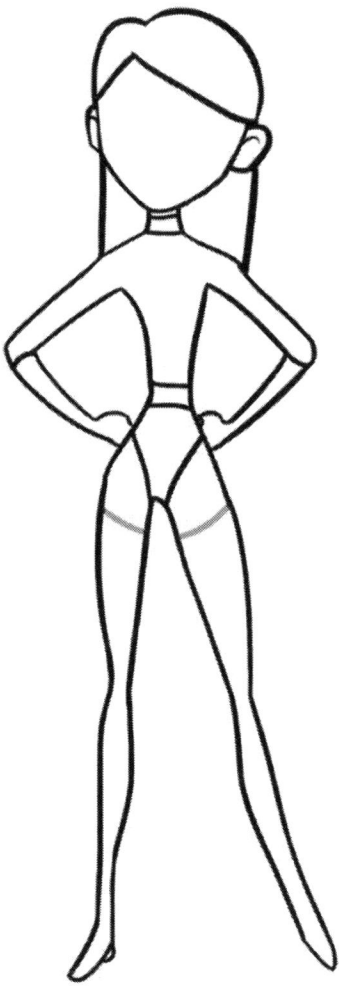

10. In the upper part of the legs we draw lines.

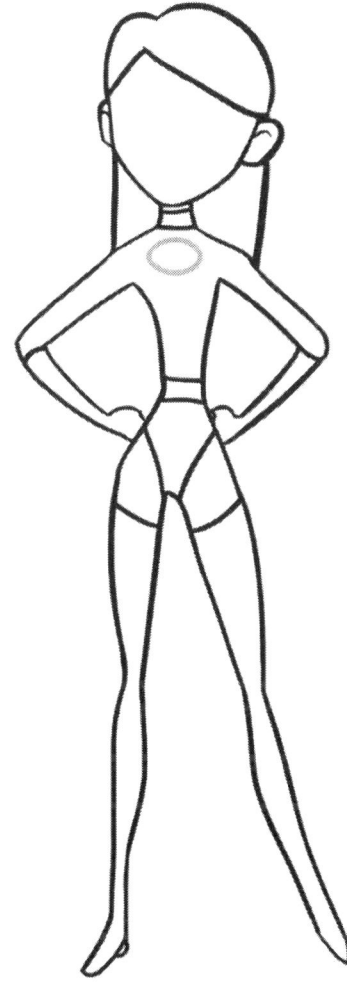

11. For the emblem, draw a horizontal oval shape.

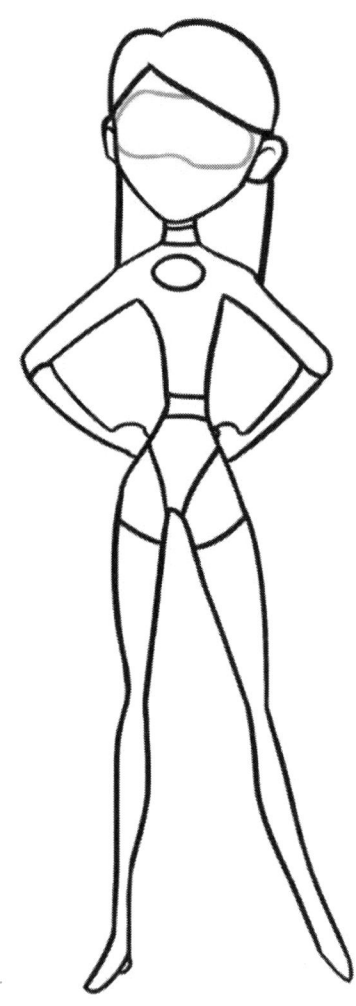

12. Inside the head, draw a rectangular shape. It will be a mask.

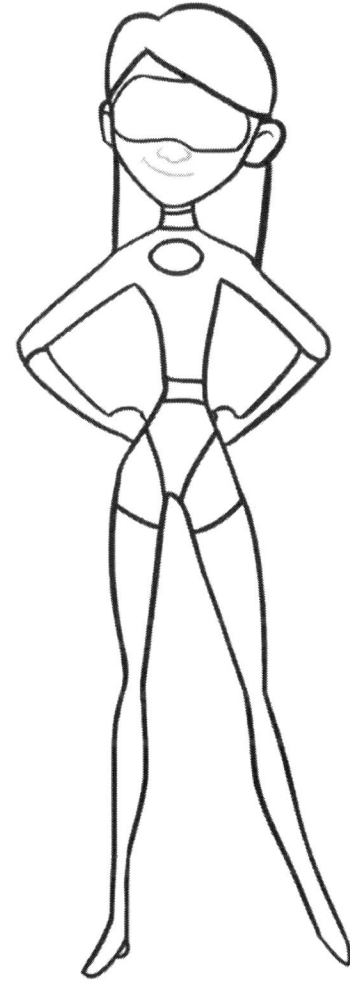

13. Below the mask, draw a curved line of the nose. Below the nose draw a horizontal line of the mouth.

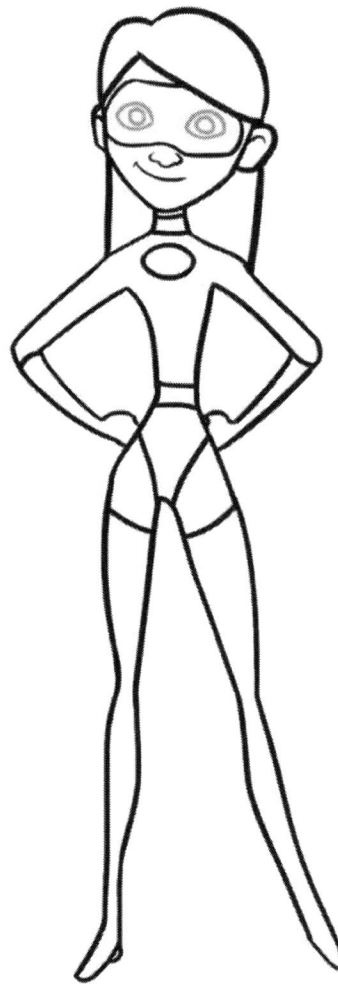

14. For the eyes, draw a horizontal oval shape inside which we draw a circular shape of the pupil. Repeat the same for the second eye.

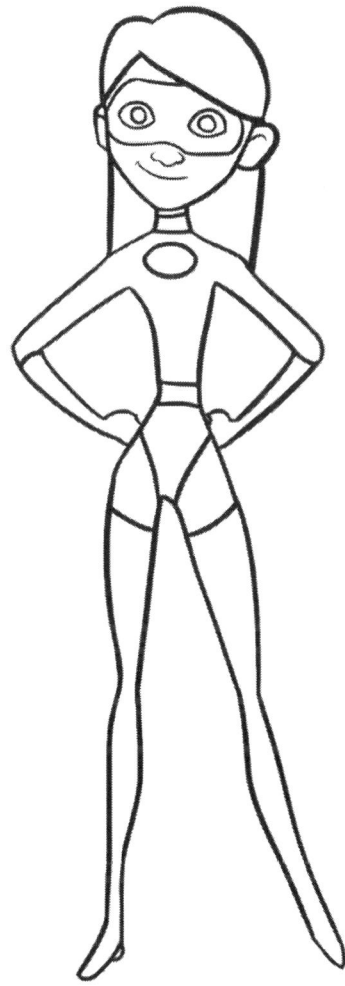

15. Done! Great job. Now go to the color.

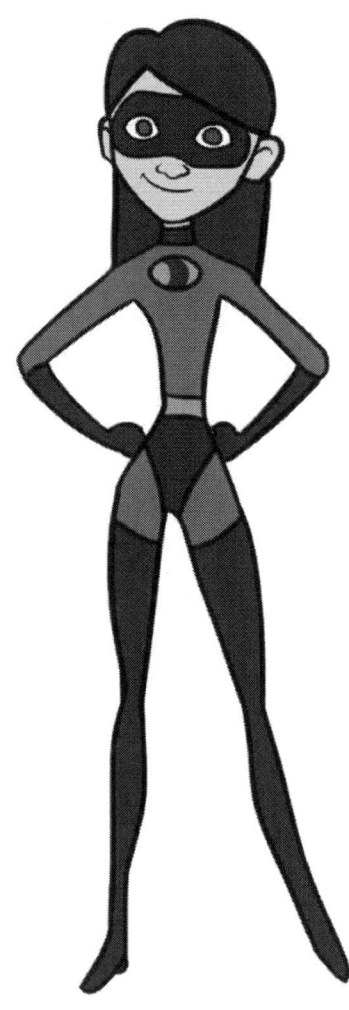

16. Body of Violet is light pink, clothes are red-black, hair is black.

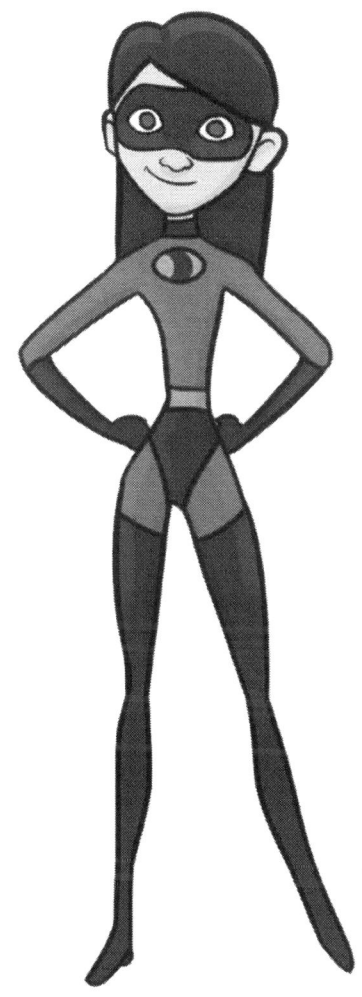

17. Next we add shadows and light to make Violet volumetric.

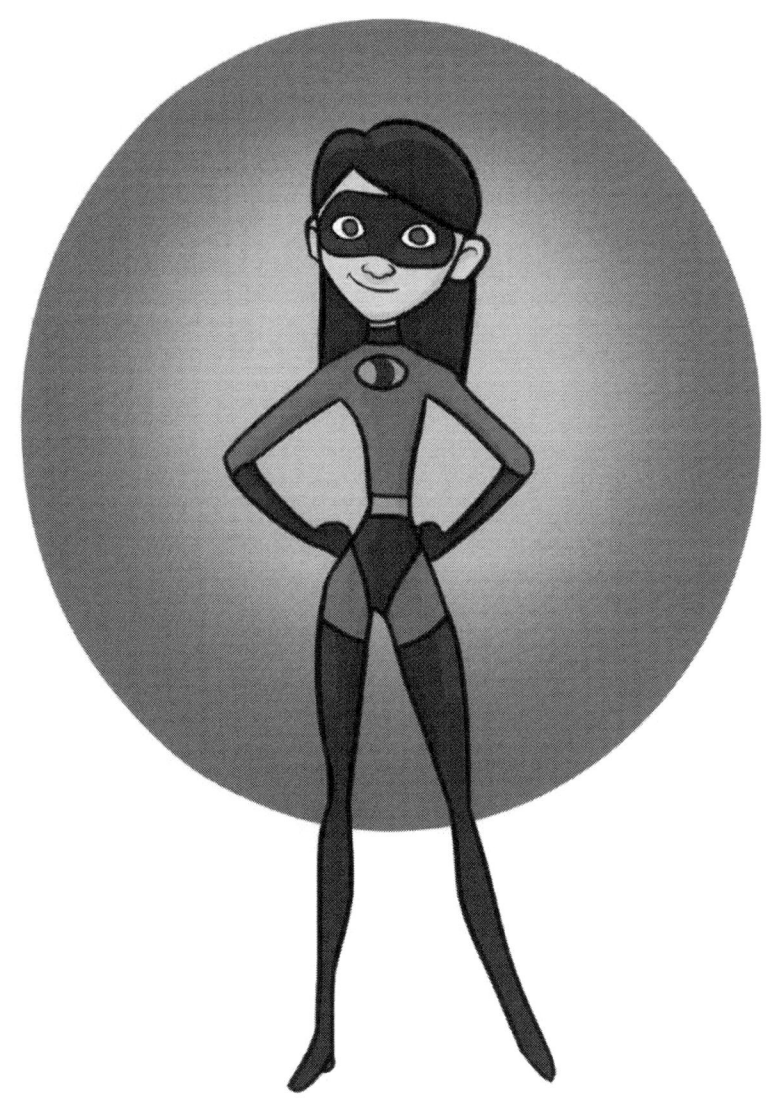

18. Colored version

How to draw Dash

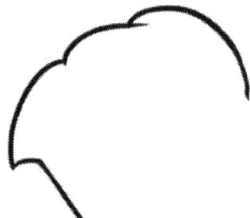

1. Draw three connected oval forms. It will be the hair.

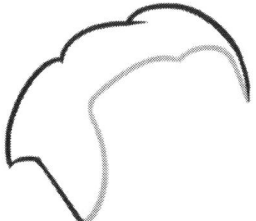

2. Inside we draw two connected arcs.

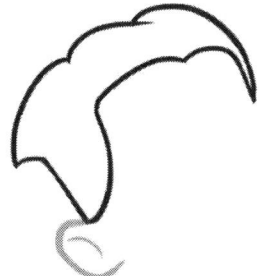

3. Drawing the ear. To do this, we draw an arc from the left, drawing an arc of a smaller size.

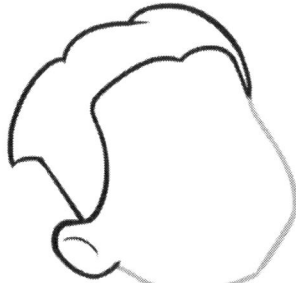

4. We connect the ear with the hair line. To do this, draw an oval face line.

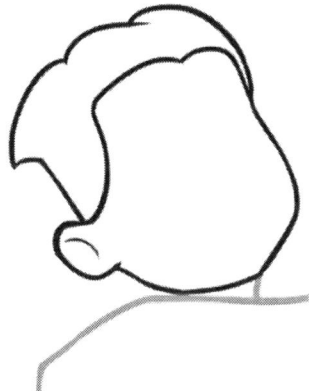

5. Below our heads draw a short vertical line and a horizontal line of shoulders.

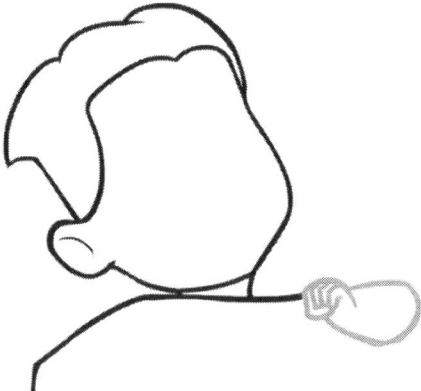

6. On the right, we draw two connected rectangular forms.
Inside less form draw four arcs. It will be a hand.

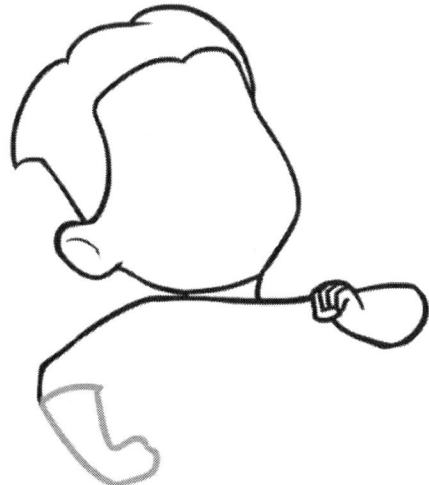

7. On the left, we draw a curved rectangular shape of the second hand.

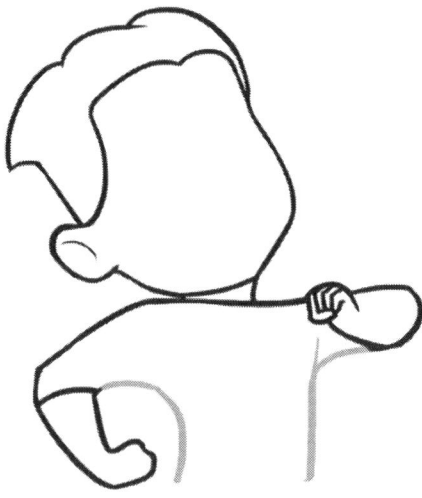

8. Draw from the hands of the arc which will be the body.

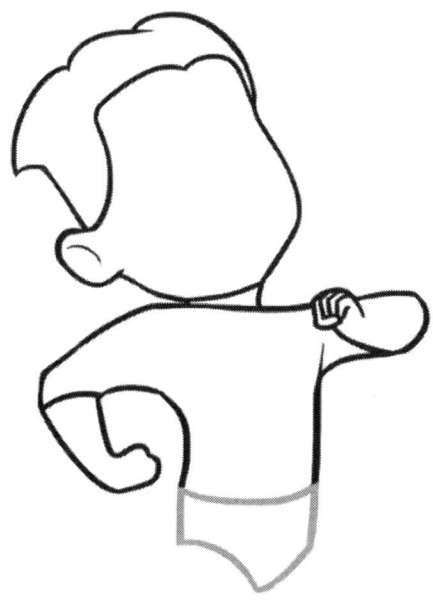

9. We connect the arcs with a horizontal line. From this line down we draw two vertical lines. Below we draw two connected arcs.

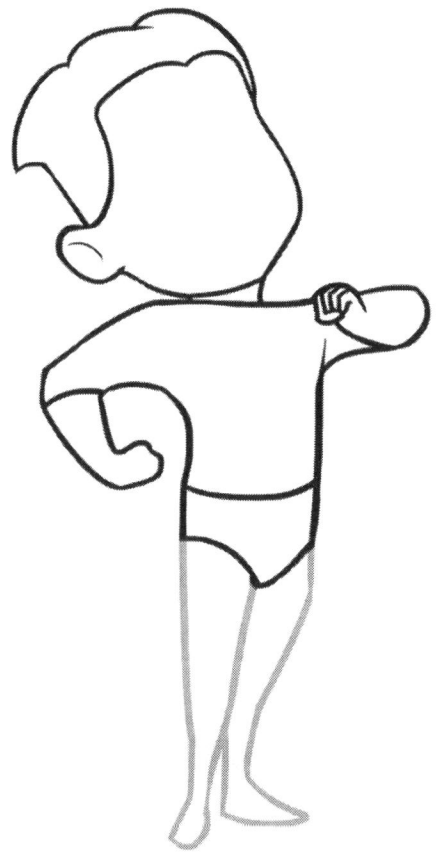

10. Draw two rectangular shapes connected at the end.
It will be legs.

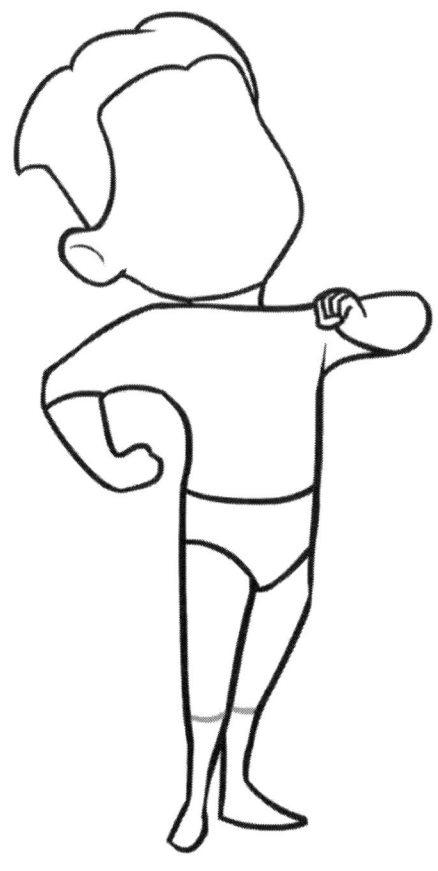

11. In the lower part of the legs we draw horizontal lines.
This is the line of shoes.

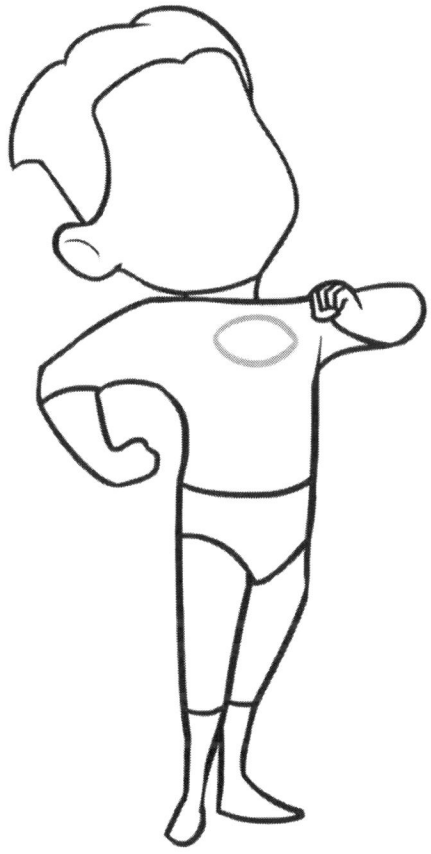

12. For the emblem, draw a horizontal oval shape.

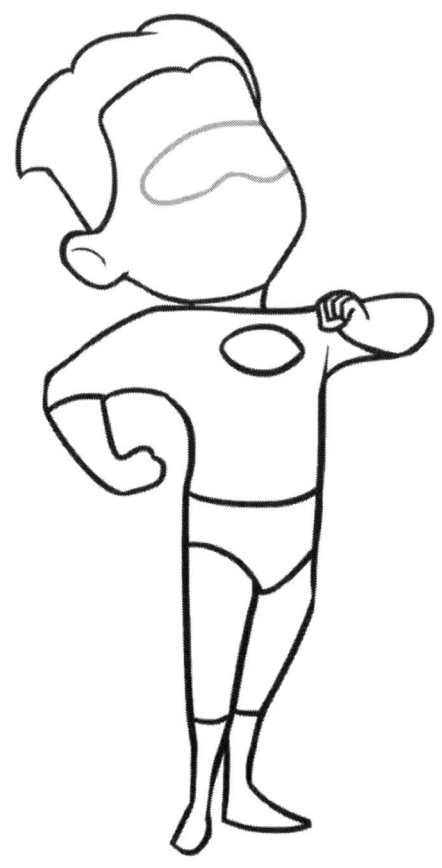

13. Inside the head, draw a horizontal oval shape. It will be a mask.

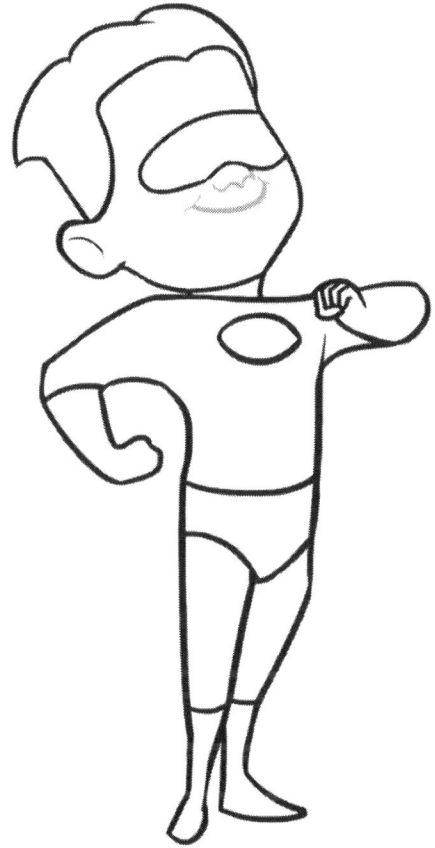

14. Below the mask draw curved lines for the nose. Below the nose, draw the arc ends that point upward. It will be a mouth.

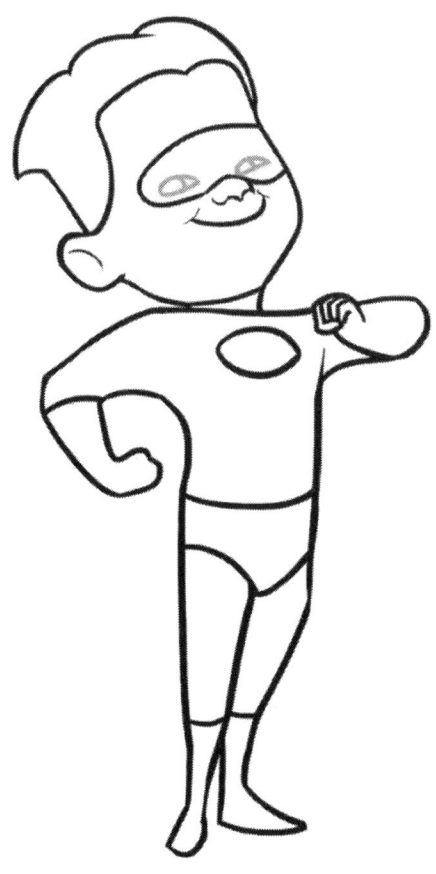

15. For the eyes, draw a horizontal oval shape inside each shape and draw a vertical arc.

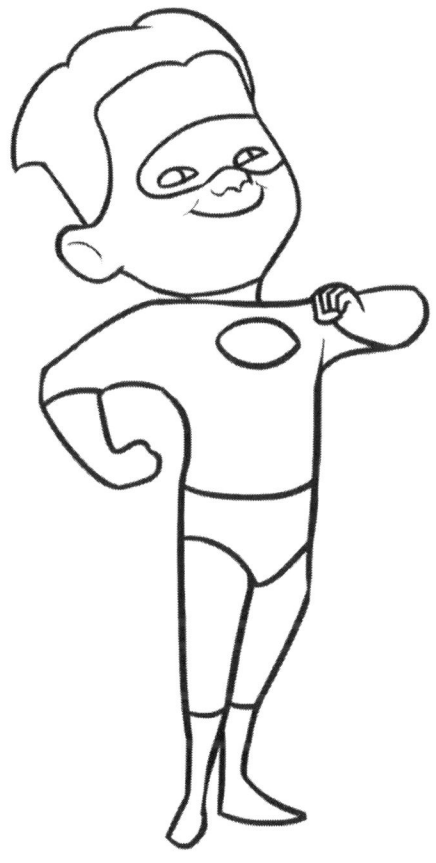

16. Done! Great job. Now go to the color.

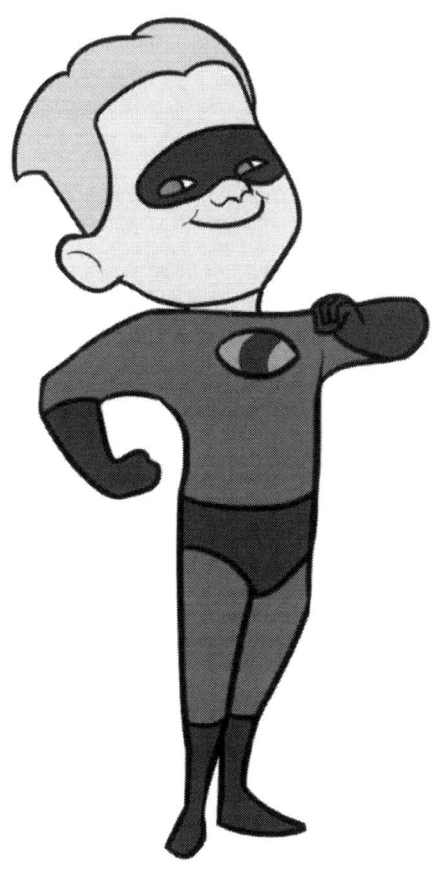

17. Dash's body is light pink, his clothes are red and black, his hair is yellow.

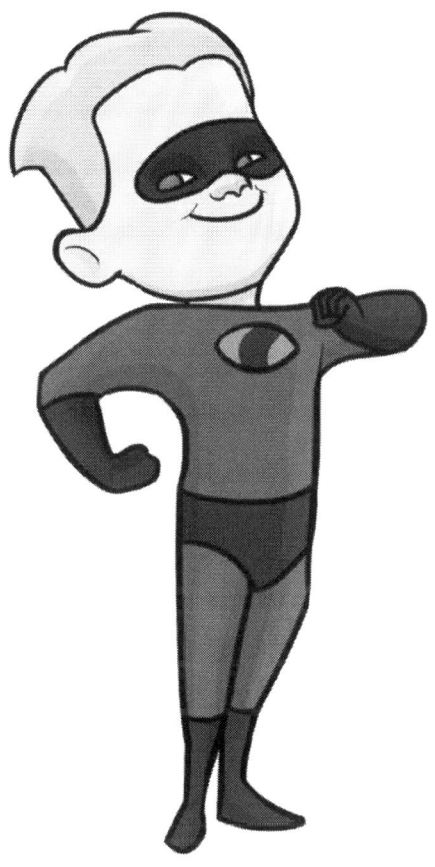

18. Next, we add shadows and light to make Dash volumetric.

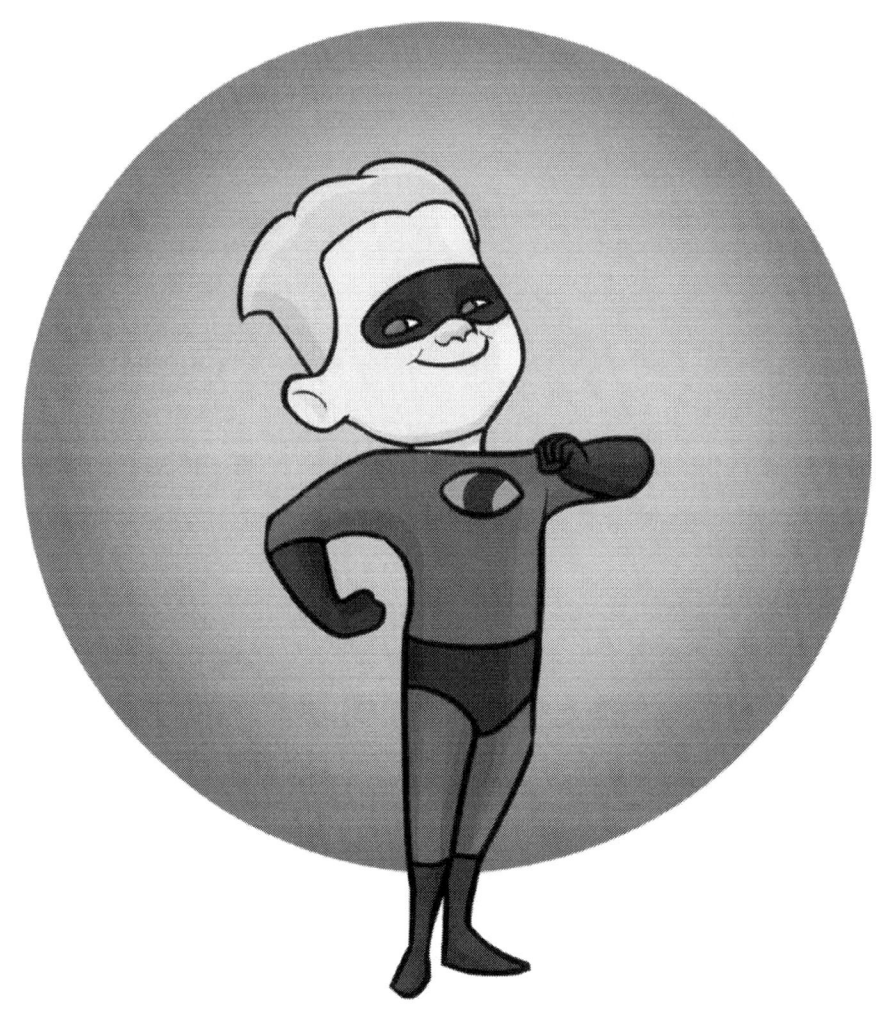

19. Colored version

How to draw Jack-Jack Parr

1. Draw a triangular shape. It will be the hair.

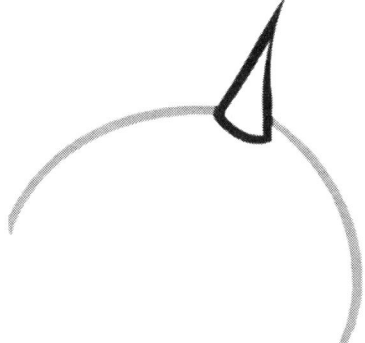

2. Right and left of the hair draw an arc. It will be a head.

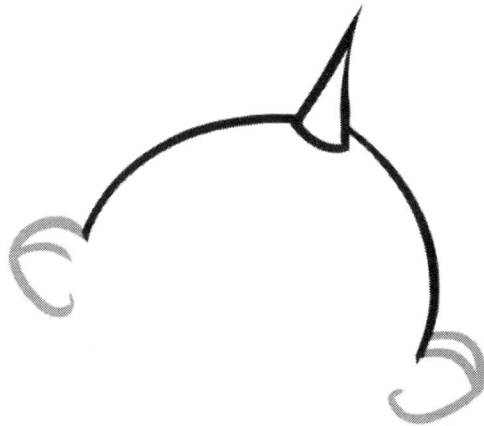

3. Drawing ears. For this, on the right and left, draw a circular shape inside which we draw an arc.

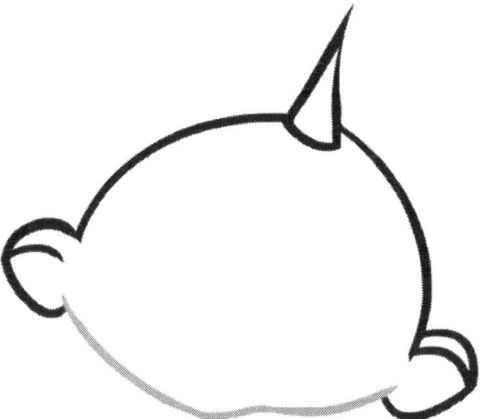

4. We connect the ears with the help of an arc.

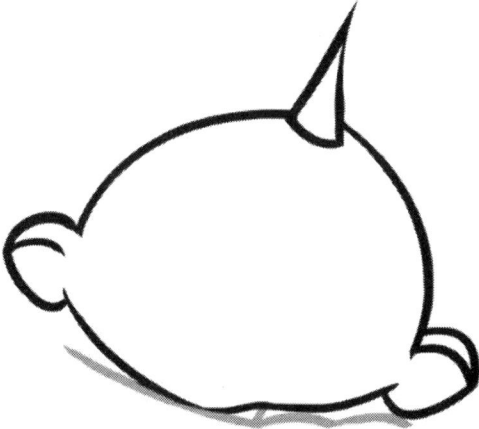

5. Draw a horizontal line. These will be the lines of hands.

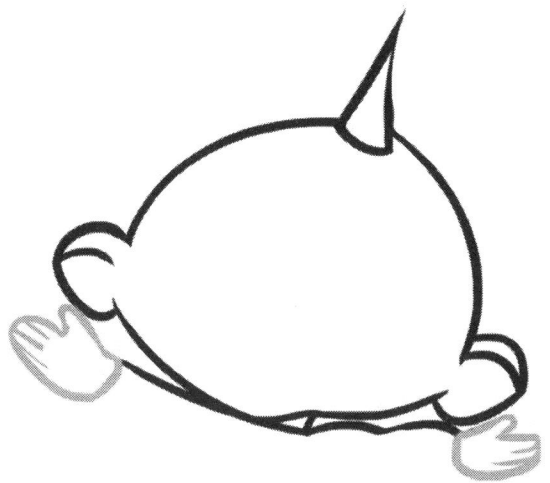

6. On the right and on the left we draw palms. To do this, draw two connected oval forms. Inside the larger form we hold 4 lines.

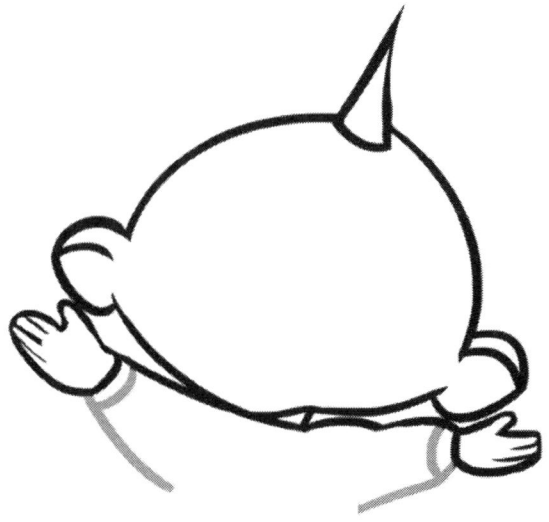

7. Down from the palms we draw a line. Below the palms draw horizontal arcs.

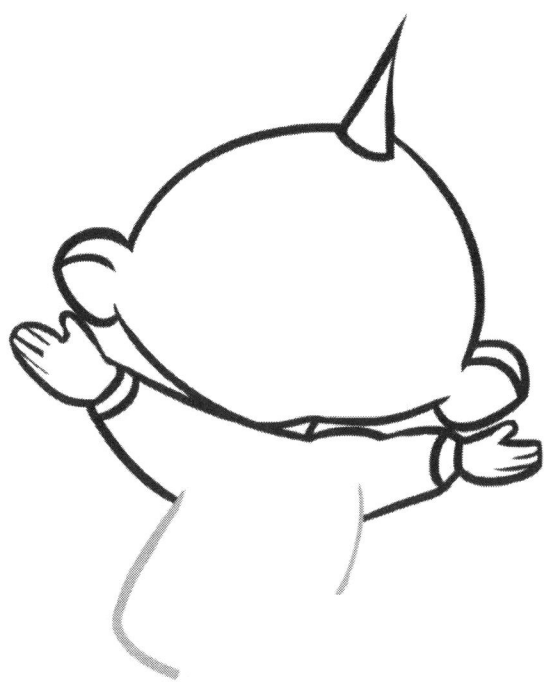

8. Add two arcs that will be the body.

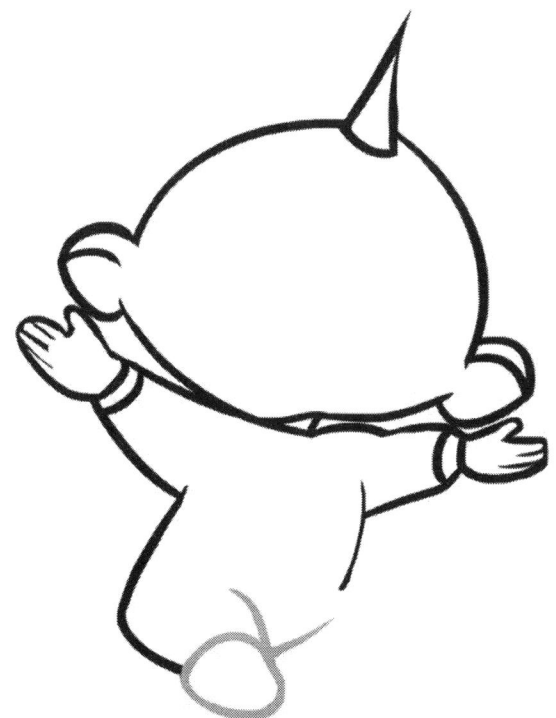

9. Draw the circular shape on the left. Up from this form, draw two connected at the beginning of the arc.

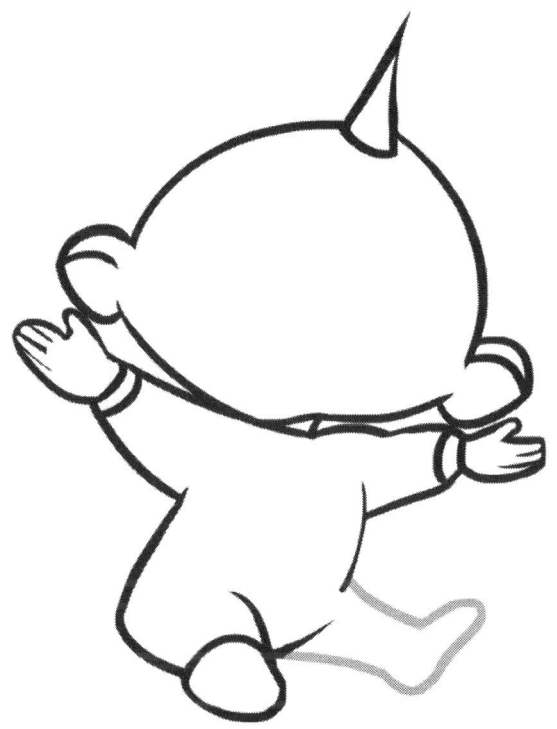

10. On the right, we draw a rectangular shape that connects to the body with two parallel lines. This will be the second leg.

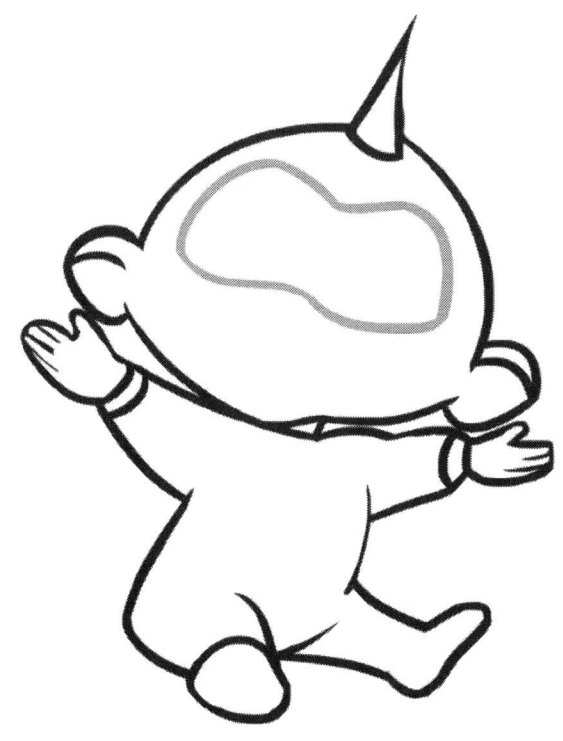

11. Inside the head, draw a horizontal rectangular shape.
It will be a mask.

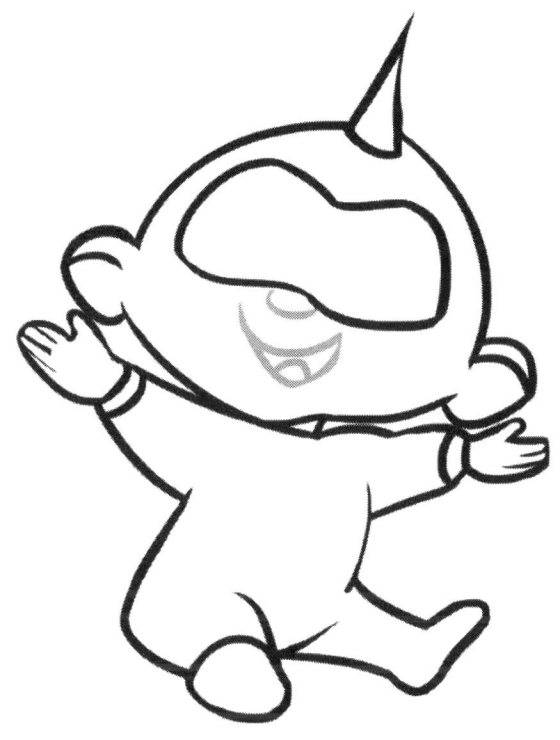

12. Below the mask draw an arc. It will be a nose.
Below the nose draw two arcs connected at the ends. Inside the formed form, draw an arc. It will be a mouth.

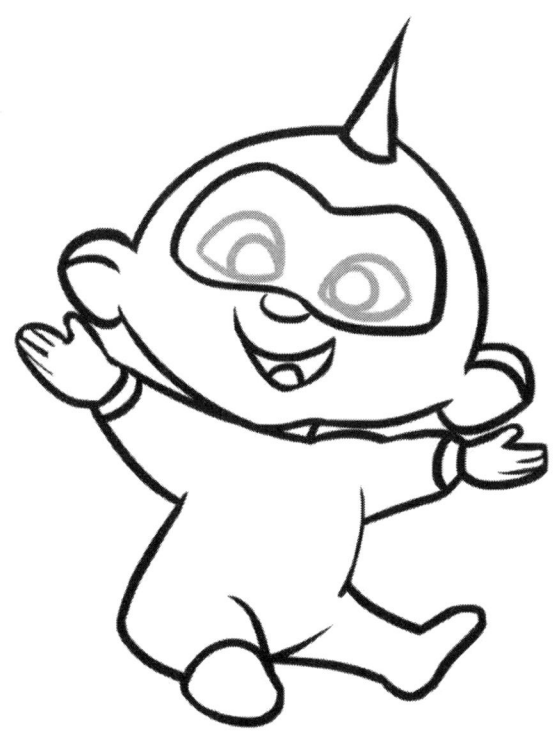

13. To draw an eye inside the oval horizontal shapes draw a round shape. The same way we draw the second eye.

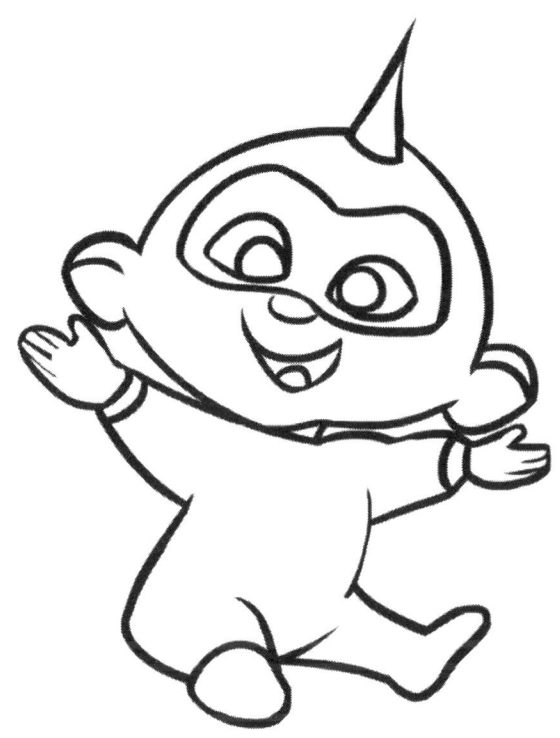

14. Done! Great job. Now go to the color.

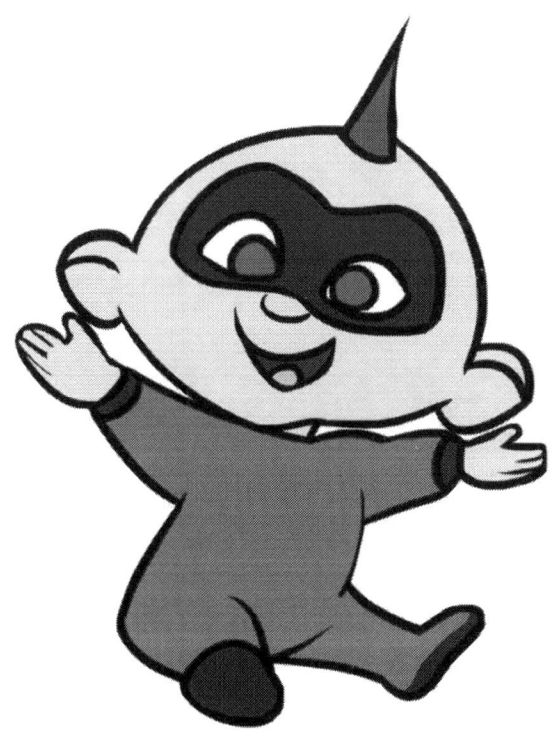

15. The body of Jack-Jack is light pink, the clothes are red-black, the hair is brown.

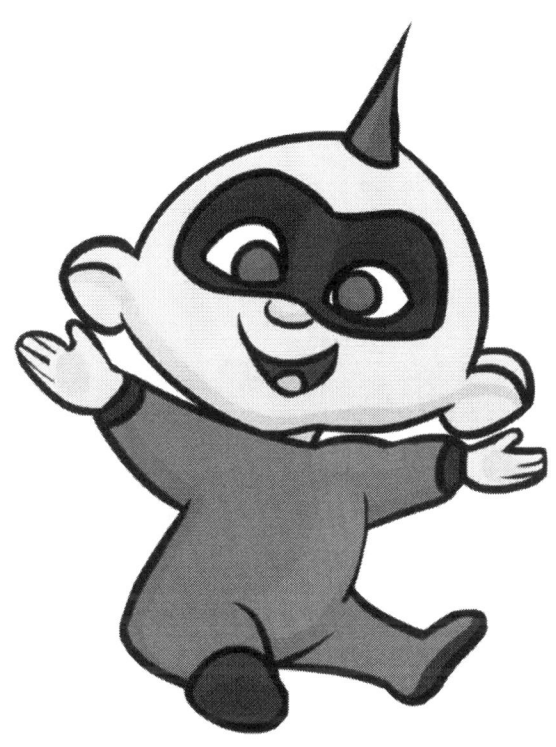

16. Next, we add shadows and light to make Jack-Jack voluminous.

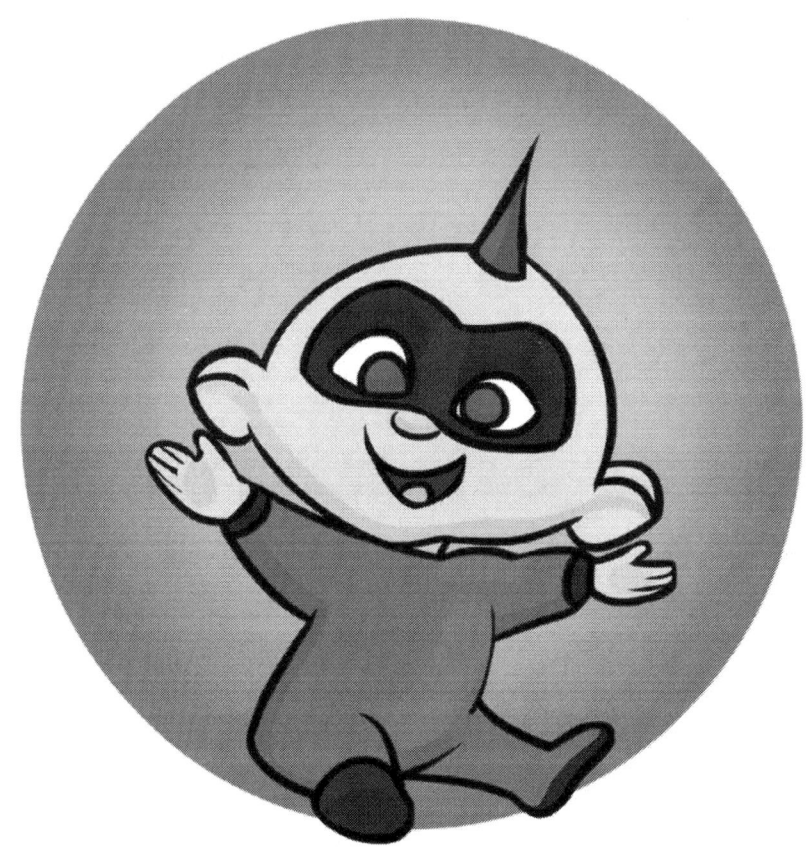

17. Colored version

How to draw Mirage

1. Draw two connected triangular forms. It will be the hair.

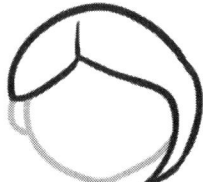

2. On the left we draw an ear. For this we draw an arc.
We connect the hair lines with an oval arc. It will be a head.

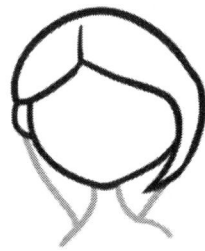

3. Below our heads draw two curved lines. These will be the lines of the neck and shoulders. We connect the lines of shoulders and hair with vertical lines.

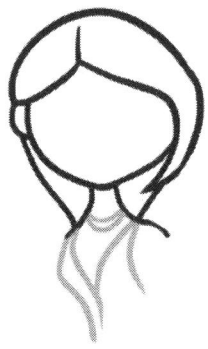

4. We connect the neck lines with two parallel arcs.
It will be a decoration. Below we draw two interconnected triangular forms.
It will be a dress.

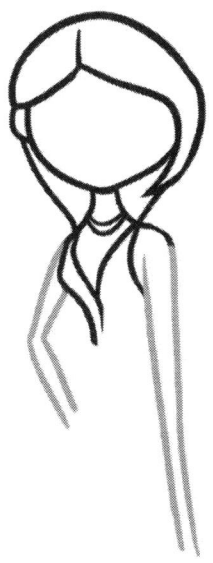

5. On the right, we draw two parallel straight lines. On the left, draw two curved parallel lines. It will be hands.

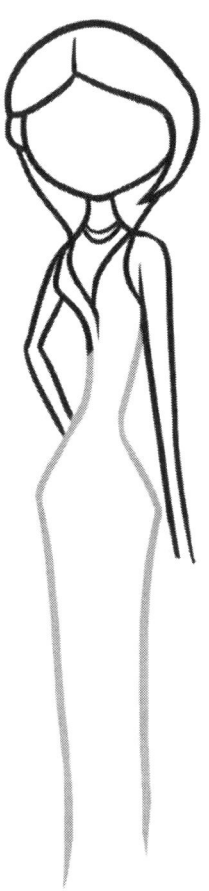

6. Draw two zigzag lines. It will be a dress.

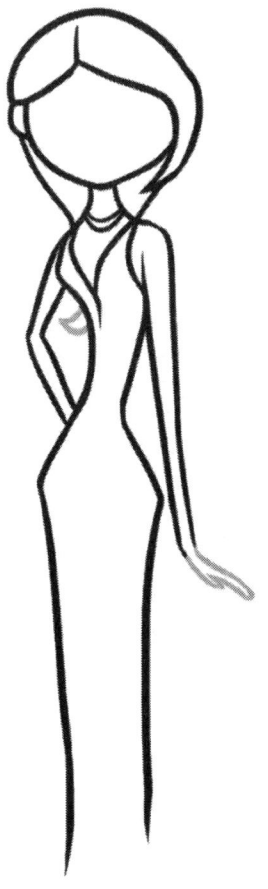

7. On the right, we draw two rectangular connected forms. This will be the palm of hand. On the left we add a triangular shape of hair.

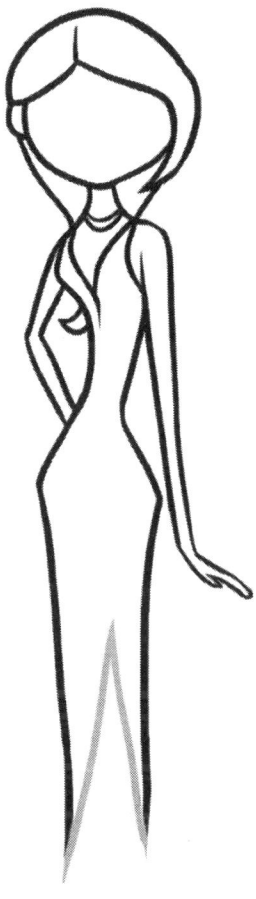

8. Draw two straight lines connected together in the beginning.

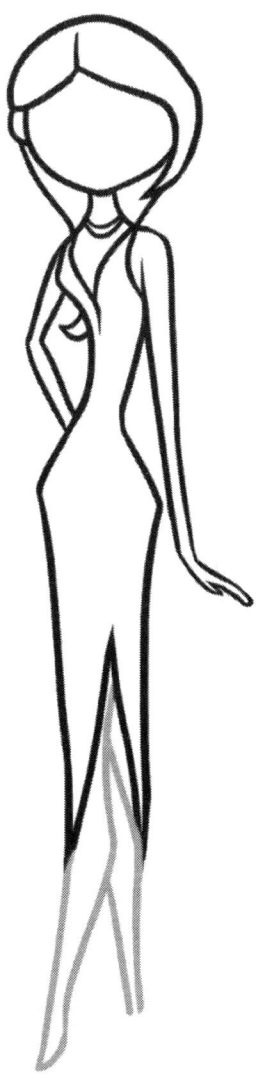

9. Draw four curved lines that will be legs.

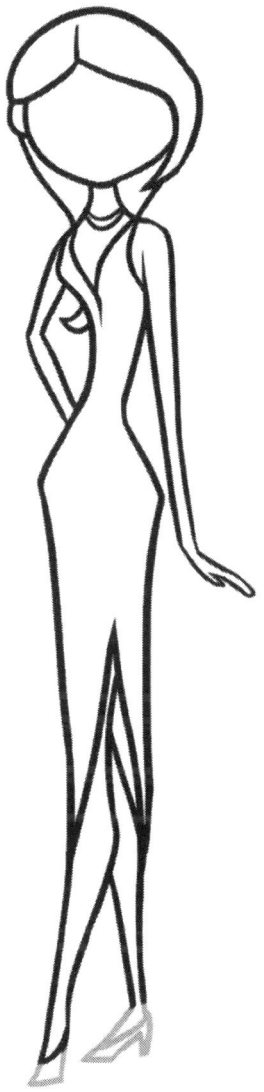

10. On the left we draw a rectangular shape. On the right, we draw two connected rectangular forms. It will be shoes.

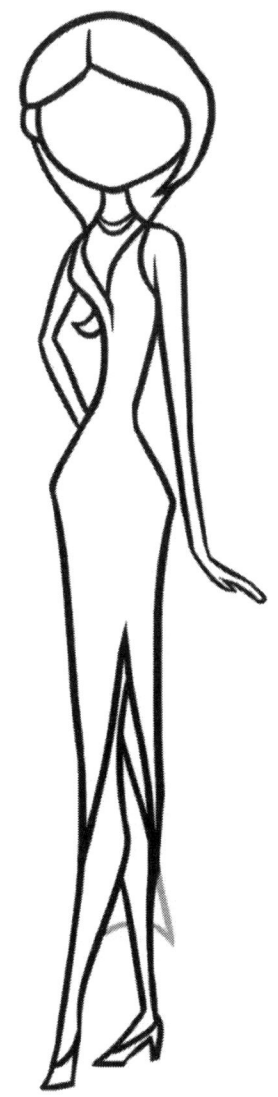

11. Add 3 lines of dress.

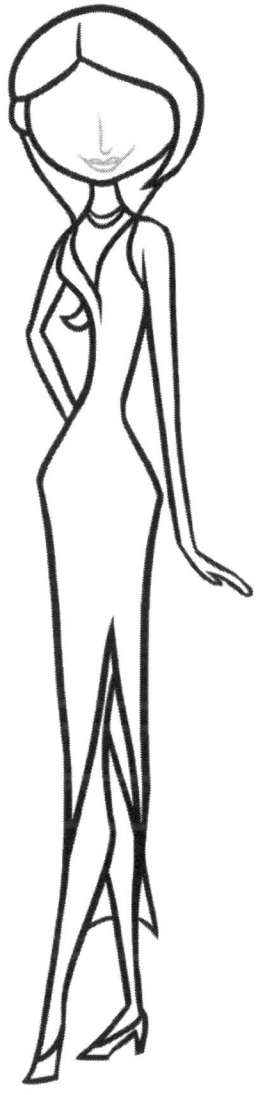

12. For the nose, draw a straight rounded end. To draw a mouth draw three connected at each end of the arc.

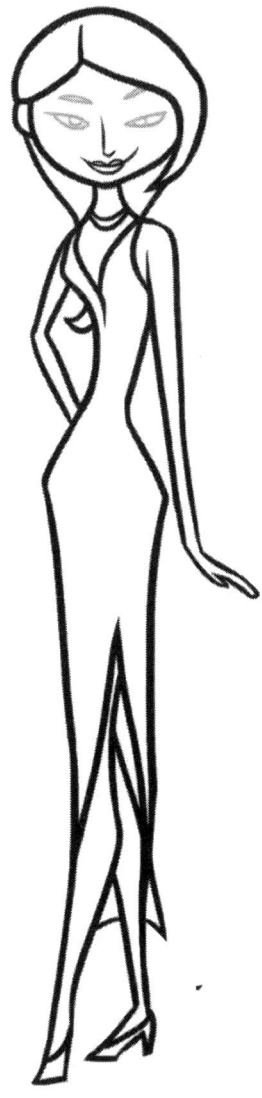

13. For the eyes, we draw triangular shapes inside which we draw round shapes. Above the eyes we draw eyebrows.

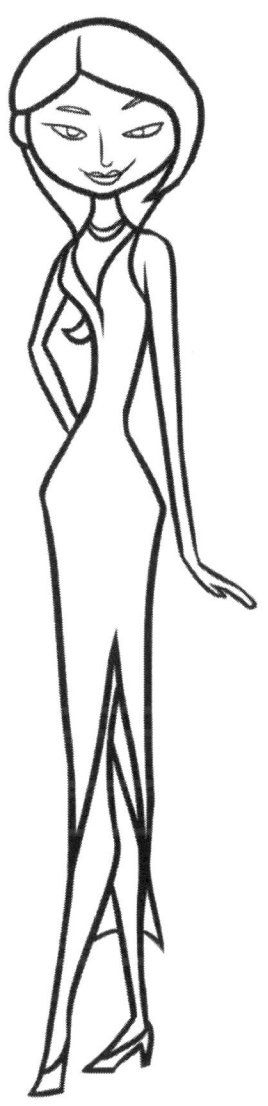

14. Done! Great job. Now go to the color.

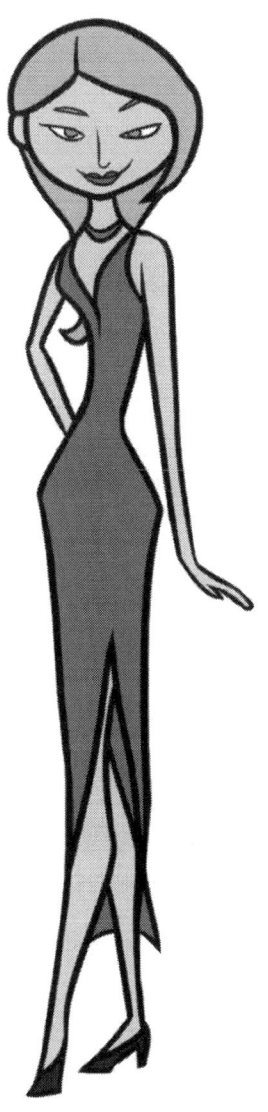

15. Body of Mirage is pink, dress violet, hair gray.

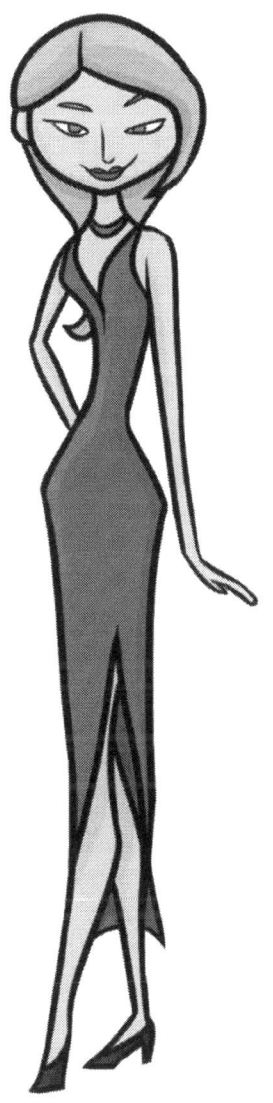

16. Next, we add shadows and light to make the Mirage voluminous.

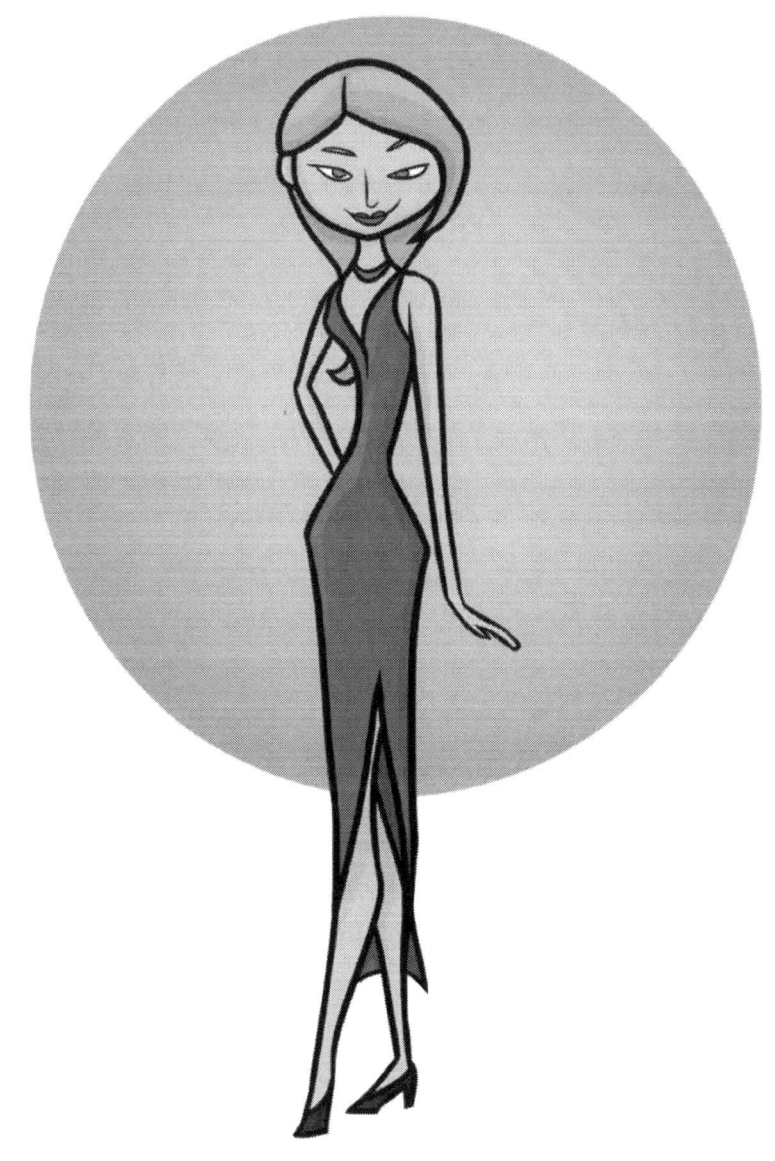

17. Colored version

How to draw Edna Mode

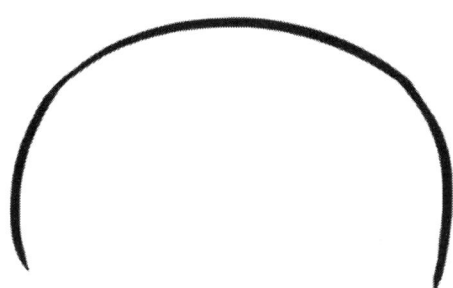

1. Draw the arc ends that are pointing down. It will be the hair.

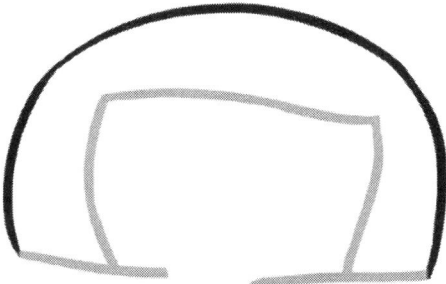

2. Draw inside a rectangular shape at the ends of which we draw horizontal lines.

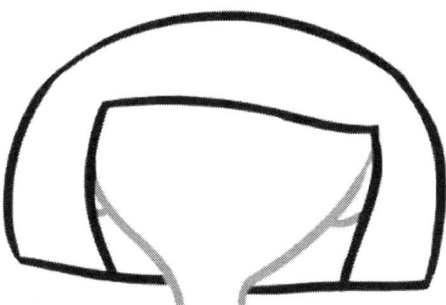

3. Draw two curved arcs that will be face. To the right and left of the face we hold arches of ears.

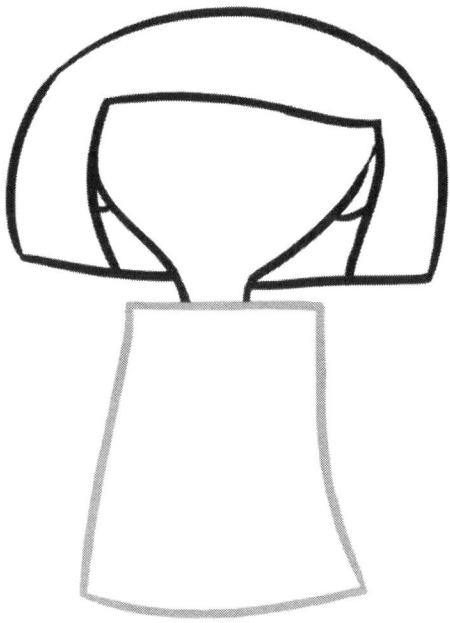

4. Below we draw a rectangular vertical shape. It will be clothes.

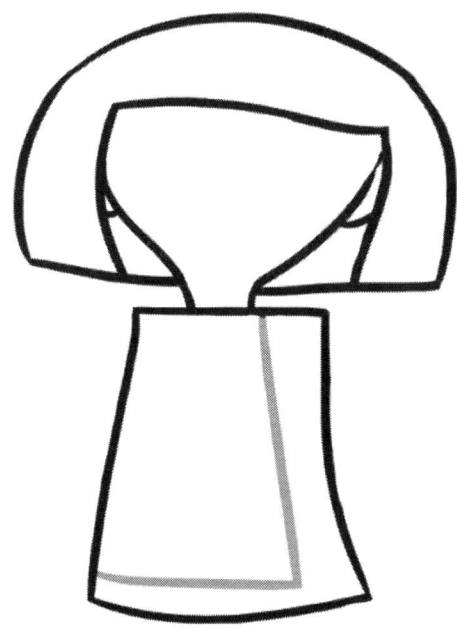

5. Inside we draw two perpendicular lines connected together.

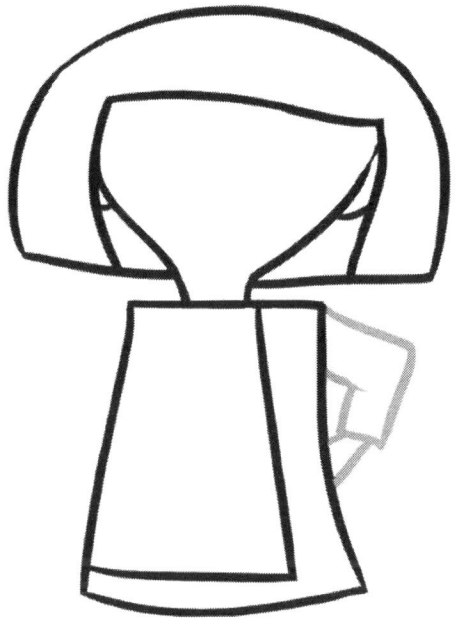

6. On the right we draw a hand. To do this, we connect two rectangular forms. Below, draw two lines connected to the body.

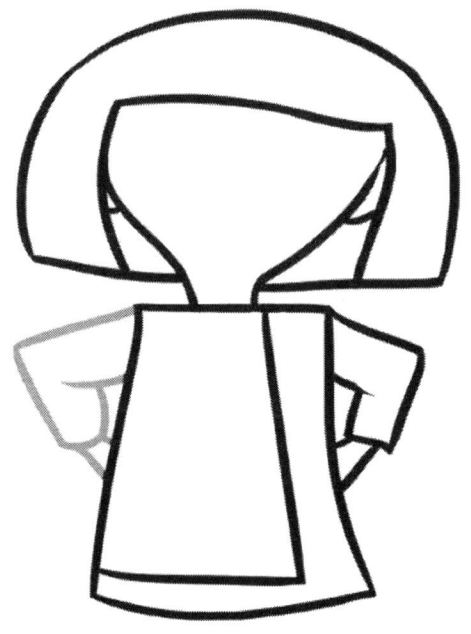

7. In the same way, draw the second hand on the left.

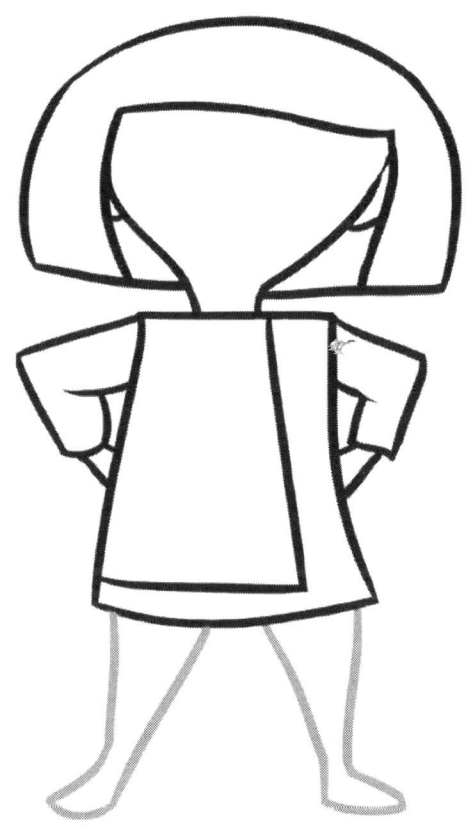

8. Draw four vertical lines that end in rectangular shapes. It will be legs.

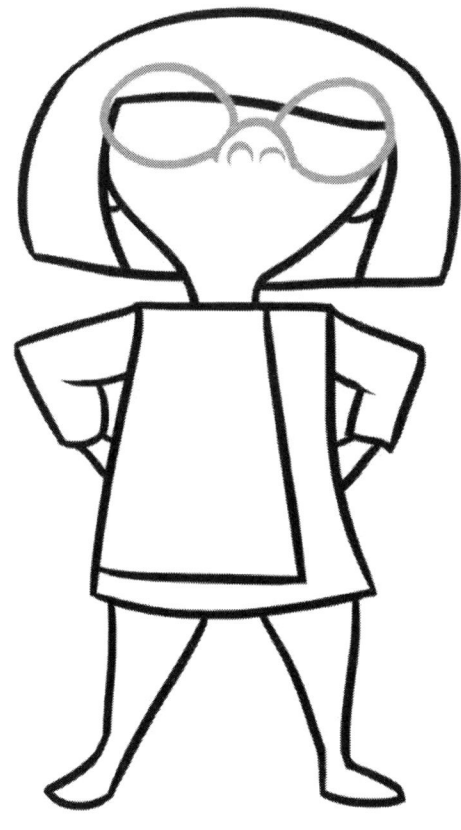

9. Draw two round shapes on the head. It will be glasses. In the center of the glasses draw an arc whose ends are directed down. Inside this arc draw two arcs the size smaller. It will be a nose.

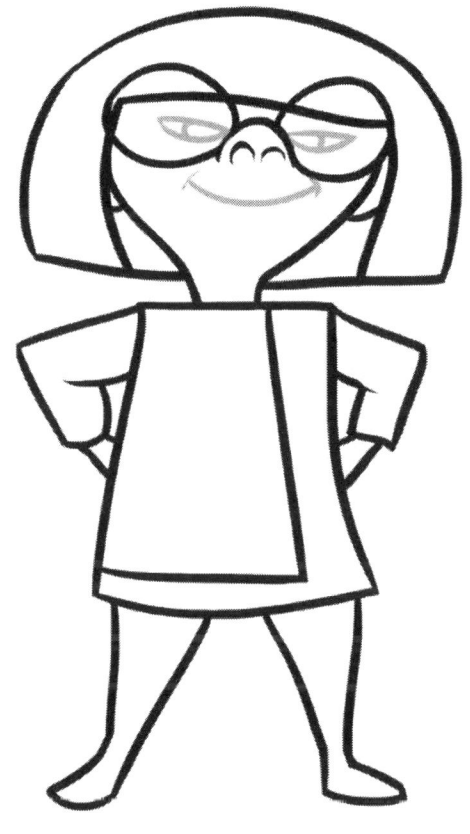

10. Draw the arc whose ends are directed upwards.
It will be a mouth. For the eyes, draw two connected at the ends
of the horizontal lines. Inside the formed shapes, draw a short vertical arc.

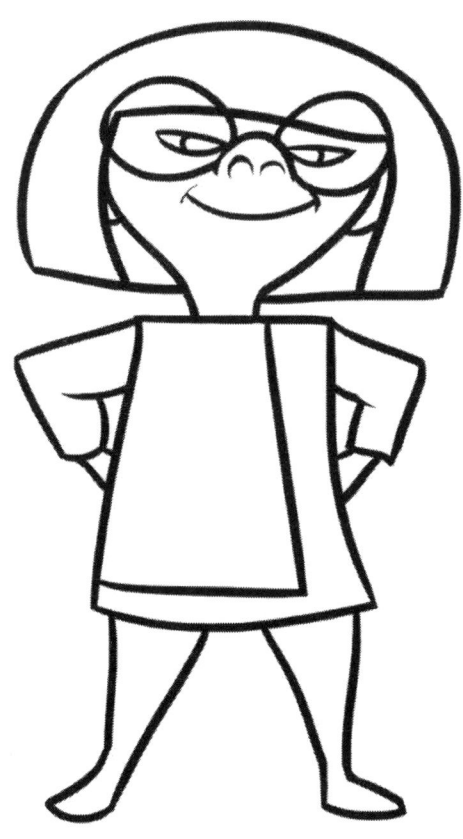

11. Done! Great job. Now go to the color.

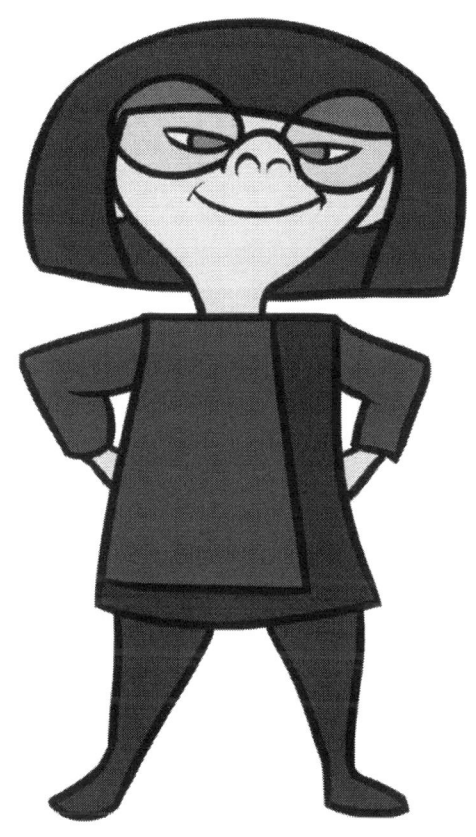

12. Edna's body Ocher colors, blue-black clothes, black hair.

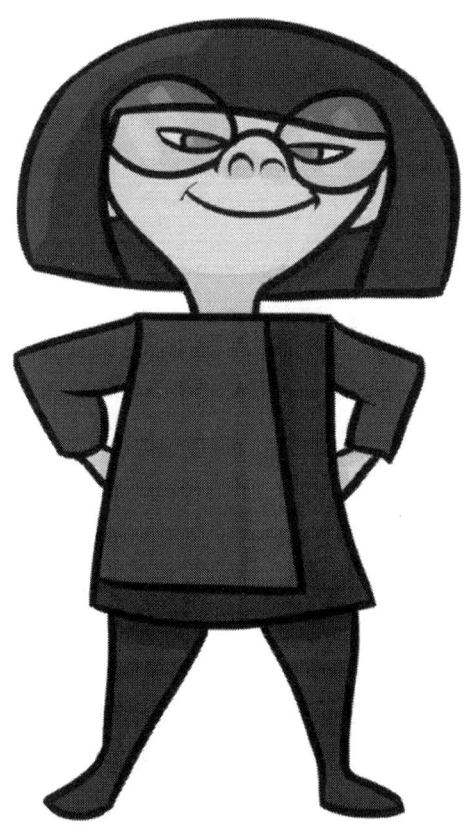

13. Next, we add shadows and light to make Edna voluminous.

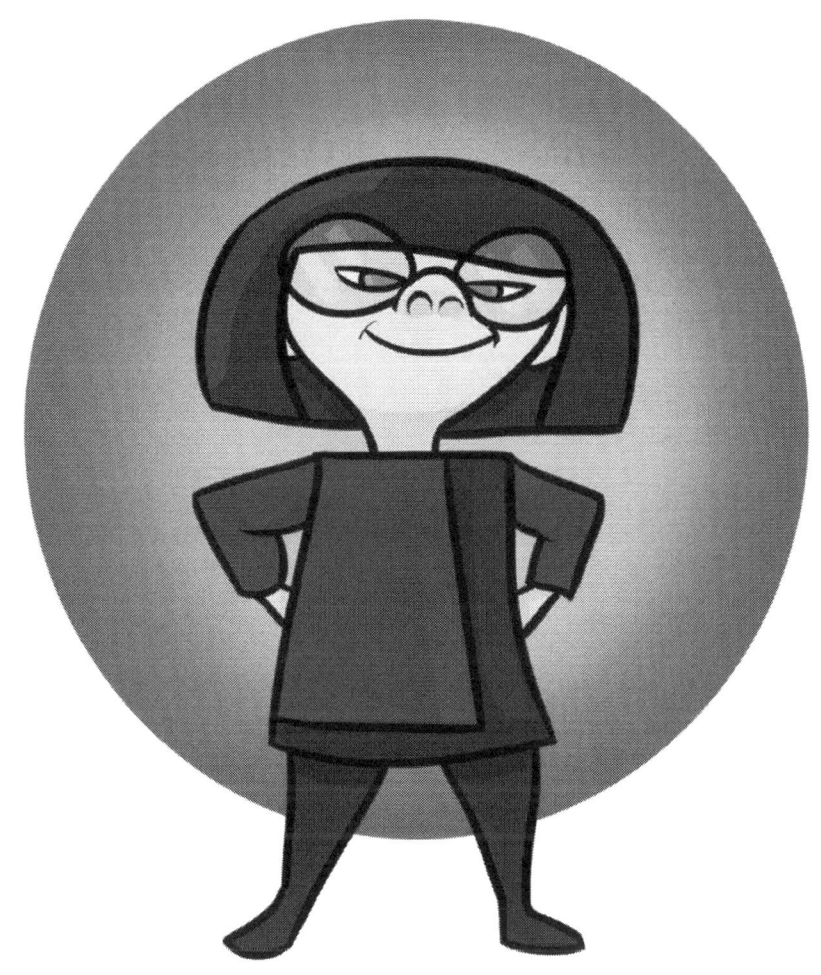

14. Colored version

Made in the USA
San Bernardino, CA
21 November 2018